CRISIS NEGOTIATION FOR LAW ENFORCEMENT, CORRECTIONS, AND EMERGENCY SERVICES

ABOUT THE AUTHOR

Dr. Arthur Slatkin is a retired police and criminal psychologist in Louisville, Kentucky. He earned his Doctorate in Counseling Psychology from the University of Louisville in 1997. His professional work in psychology has been broad and varied. He has worked in the county jail, state corrections, and at the Louisville Metro Police Department, serving since 1986 as psychologist/mental health consultant on the hostage negotiation team. As an active member of the team, he has responded to hundreds of callouts involving hostage, barricade, and suicidal persons.

Dr. Slatkin trained at the FBI Academy in Quantico, Virginia, at the FBI's local field office, and with the NYPD pioneers of hostage negotiations, Harvey Schlossberg and Frank Bolz. He is the author of *Communication in Crisis and Hostage Negotiations* and *Training Strategies in Crisis and Hostage Negotiations* as well as numerous articles on hostage negotiations in several law enforcement publications.

CRISIS NEGOTIATION FOR LAW ENFORCEMENT, CORRECTIONS, AND EMERGENCY SERVICES

Crisis Intervention as Crisis Negotiation

By

ARTHUR SLATKIN, Ed.D

Police and Criminal Psychology
Louisville Metro Police Department/Hostage Negotiation Team
Louisville, Kentucky

CHARLES C THOMAS • PUBLISHER, LTD.
Springfield • Illinois • U.S.A.

Published and Distributed Throughout the World by

CHARLES C THOMAS • PUBLISHER, LTD.
2600 South First Street
Springfield, Illinois 62704

This book is protected by copyright. No part of
it may be reproduced in any manner without written
permission from the publisher. All rights reserved

© 2015 by CHARLES C THOMAS • PUBLISHER, LTD.

ISBN 978-0-398-09065-4 (paper)
ISBN 978-0-398-09066-1 (ebook)

Library of Congress Catalog Card Number: 2014048632

With THOMAS BOOKS *careful attention is given to all details of manufacturing and design. It is the Publisher's desire to present books that are satisfactory as to their physical qualities and artistic possibilities and appropriate for their particular use.* THOMAS BOOKS *will be true to those laws of quality that assure a good name and good will.*

Printed in the United States of America
SM-R-3

Library of Congress Cataloging-in-Publication Data

Slatkin, Arthur A.
  Crisis negotiation for law enforcement, corrections, and emergency services : crisis intervention as crisis negotiation / by Arthur Slatkin.
     pages cm
  Includes bibliographical references.
  ISBN 978-0-398-09065-4 (pbk.) -- ISBN 978-0-398-09066-1 (ebook)
  1. Hostage negotiations. 2. Crisis management. 3. Communication in law enforcement. I Title.
  HV6595.5533 2015
  363.23-dc23

2014048632

To the scores of officers of the Louisville Metro Police Department who have served on the Hostage Negotiation Team over the years of my tenure.

To my family for their love and support.

PREFACE

Crisis Negotiation, the third of three volumes, is meant to follow from the first two in a logic of my choosing. The first, *Communication in Crisis and Hostage Negotiation*, highlighted effective communication as the foundation of any human interaction, and the absolute keystone to crisis negotiations; the second book, *Training Strategies for Crisis Negotiations*, proffered a variety of training means and modes to develop skills and practice for operational effectiveness. This current book focuses on operational theory and practice for Negotiators by following a crisis intervention model for crisis negotiations.

Crisis Negotiation for Law Enforcement, Corrections, and Emergency Services: Crisis Intervention as Crisis Negotiation is the third in a series of handbooks principally for law enforcement, corrections, and emergency service Negotiators. My intention is to provide some depth and breadth of understanding for instructors, students, and, ultimately, line negotiators seeking excellence in their professional role of *hostage/crisis* negotiator. After 28 years as a police and correctional crisis negotiator and consultant, I have met hundreds of Negotiators; nearly none of them have any understanding of the roots, underpinnings, foundation, or structure of crisis intervention, the basis of crisis negotiations. In fairness to them, they have never been taught about it by those who had never themselves been taught it. For them, hostage negotiations is a stand-alone "thing" they do and from whence it comes is not their concern. Oddly, it has not hampered generations of police negotiators overall – their records of success are enviable. So why care? Why not leave well enough alone? You can't argue with success. If it ain't broke, why fix it?

Simply put, this book may not be for everyone – there are journeymen Negotiators who are "good enough" in most cases – but, I believe that those Negotiators who know more, and know more in depth and breadth what they are doing and why they are doing it, can apply their greater understanding of human behavior to be better than good enough. The real amalgam of art and the science of the field of crisis negotiations is knowledge in depth and its skillful, practical application in aid of others. This book is for those who want to be much more than just good enough; sometimes good enough is not enough.

Hostage Negotiations, as a law enforcement strategy, was introduced by Dr. Harvey Schlossberg, a working police detective and trained psychologist at the NYPD, after a spate of high-profile local and international incidents turned out badly, challenging police to develop more effective and life-preserving responses to high-profile and mundane public crises. Police tactics had been limited to violent tactical assault. Inevitably, when police kicked in a door, there were casualties – officers, hostages, bystanders, Subjects. In recognition of a failed one-option tactic, police officials tasked Dr. Schlossberg to develop an alternative strategy. Hostage negotiations was born of a mix of the wisdom from law enforcement experience and psychological principles; the strategies, tactics, and techniques developed by Dr. Schlossberg are grounded in sound police and psychological sciences and practices. Captain Frank Bolz, also of the NYPD, and his ESU teams field tested the new approaches.

Dr. Schlossberg has described the actions of hostage takers (barricaded Subjects, and public suicide-threateners) as "maladaptive," that is, in an effort to cope with changing life circumstances, personal and external events, and demanding and stressful situations, a Subject attempts to maintain equilibrium or balance. In so doing, a person chooses a way or means that is unhelpful, makes things worse, or fails because of his or her poor judgment. People's actions, and the poor judgment underlying, can be self-injurious, homicidal, or irrational. They may have turned a misdemeanor into a felony, so-to-speak. Clearly, it becomes the realm of both law enforcement officers *and* mental health professionals; each brings experience, expertise, and in the case of the police, a legal mandate to act in regard to breaches of public order.

Early on, a jurisdictional dispute arose among the two camps – the police and the mental health professional community; each saw their expertise as more expert! In the end, the legal mandate could not be abridged nor traded off and so, law enforcement remained in charge of crisis management. Mental Health Professionals (MHP) were relegated largely to training police in grounded psychological and crisis intervention theory and practice. MHP bring a winning strategy – Crisis Negotiation – a derivative of the successful Crisis Intervention treatment modality.

This book, like the other two: *Communication in Crisis and Hostage Negotiations: A Handbook for Law Enforcement, Corrections and Emergency Service Personnel in Managing Critical Incidents* and, *Training Strategies for Crisis and Hostage Negotiations: Scenario Writing and Creative Variations in Role Play*, are written principally to enhance Negotiator confidence and competence, well-grounded in the deliberate and effective use of self as an intervener and Negotiator in critical incidents.

The history of crisis negotiations should be taught and learned if negotiators are to grow the field and grow in the field. A true story: When I wrote my first book, I asked Captain Frank Bolz and Harvey Schlossberg, as I had trained briefly with both, to each write a quotable blurb to promote the book. About the ideas and content of the book, Frank wrote that "It might work in a psychologist's examining room but that that stuff wouldn't work in the dark hallway of a tenement building with a cardboard megaphone." Harvey, on the other hand, was more sanguine; he thought "it was what was needed to add to the evolving science of a new and vital field." In light of the changes you have witnessed in police science and technology and the constant striving (demands) to do more and better (often with less), I'll let you decide whether getting better at saving lives is an imperative. I believe it is.

This book, like the other two, is distilled from my many experiences: jail and prison psychologist, crisis counselor and psychotherapist, and, mostly from my 28 years as mental health consultant for the Louisville Metro Police Department's (LMPD) Hostage Negotiation Team (HNT). In the 28 years with the HNT, I responded to 12 to 15 callouts a year (do the math).

A. S.

CONTENTS

Page
Preface vii

PART I – NEGOTIATION AS CRISIS INTERVENTION, CRISIS INTERVENTION AS NEGOTIATION

Introduction 5

Chapter

1. NEGOTIATION AS CRISIS INTERVENTION, CRISIS INTERVENTION AS NEGOTIATION 9
   Crisis Intervention 9
    Roberts' Seven-Stage Crisis Intervention Model 13
    Hostage Negotiation as Crisis Intervention and Negotiation ... 15
    Differences in Crisis Intervention and Crisis Negotiation ... 18
   Summary 18

2. STAGE I: RAPIDLY ESTABLISH RAPPORT AND A COLLABORATIVE RELATIONSHIP 19
   Rapport 20
    Respectful Engagement 22
    Engagement: Tolerance, Acceptance, Suspension of Judgment, and Empathy 23
    Some Helpful Negotiator Qualities 24
   Effective Communication 25
    Voice Quality 26
    Tone 26
    Breath Control 26
    Pitch, Meter, Rate, Intensity, Fluency, Manner 27
    Loaded Words and Phrases 27
    NLP, Representative Systems, and Mimesis 28
    Lying 29

   Active Listening 31
   Suicide Prevention 33
   Use of Humor 33
   Self-Disclosure 34
   What Not to Say 35
   Signs of Rapport and Indicators of Progress 36
  Summary 38

3. STAGE II: CONDUCT CRISIS, BIOPSYCHOSOCIAL
  AND LETHALITY ASSESSMENTS 39
   Situational Incident Assessment 41
   Assessment of the Person 45
  Lethality 48
   Resistance 50
   Beyond the Content 51
  Summary 51

4. STAGE III: IDENTIFY THE MAJOR PROBLEMS OR
  CRISIS PRECIPITANTS 53
   Sample Dialog 57
  Summary 58

5. STAGE IV: EXPLORE FEELINGS AND EMOTIONS 59
   Some Considerations 61
   Active Listening 62
   Reframing 66
   Resistance 66
  Summary 67

6. STAGE V: GENERATE AND EXPLORE
  ALTERNATIVES 69
   Baseline 70
   Alternative Behavior and Options 72
   Brainstorming 73
   Sample Interventions 73
   Looking Backward, Looking Forward 74
    Sample Dialogs 75
   Giving Advice 75
   Resistance 76
   A Plan 77
  Summary 77

7. STAGE VI: DEVELOP AND IMPLEMENT AN
   ACTION PLAN...79
   Sample Dialog..83
   Summary...83

8. STAGE VII: FOLLOW-UP...85
   Summary...87

Part II – HOSTAGE, BARRICADE, AND SUICIDAL SUBJECT NEGOTIATIONS

Introduction..97

9. HOSTAGE SITUATIONS AS CRISIS NEGOTIATIONS.....................99
   Demands..101
   Negotiable versus Nonnegotiable Demands..................102
   Negotiation Strategies, Stratagems, Tactics, and Techniques.........103
   Strategies..103
   Tactics..104
   Stratagems...105
   Techniques...106
   Stockholm Syndrome.....................................107
   The Process..108
   Power and Control......................................108
   Summary..108

10. SUICIDE AND ASSAULT: DANGER TO SELF OR
    OTHERS..111
    Some Principles..115
    *Intervention Strategies for Dealing with a Suicidal or
       Homicidal Person*.....................................116
    Contracting for Safety.................................117
    Interrupt the Plan by Removing the Means...............117
    Encourage Ventilation Cautiously.......................118
    Reality versus Fantasy.................................119
    Explore Alternatives...................................120
    An Instrumental Negotiator.............................120
    Plumb Meaning and Purpose..............................121
    Reasons to Live and Die................................122
    Inculcating Hope.......................................123
    Reigniting Self-Reliance and Self-Efficacy.............123

  Power and Control................................... 125
 Summary... 125
11. **BARRICADED SUBJECT SITUATIONS**................... 127
  Considerations...................................... 128
  Further Considerations............................... 130
  Strategies and Tactics................................ 130
  Subject Strategy.................................... 134
  Power and Control................................... 134
 Summary... 135
References... 137

CRISIS NEGOTIATION FOR LAW ENFORCEMENT, CORRECTIONS, AND EMERGENCY SERVICES

PART I

NEGOTIATION AS CRISIS INTERVENTION, CRISIS INTERVENTION AS NEGOTIATION

INTRODUCTION

Over the years, instructing police and corrections officers in hostage negotiations, I have often introduced my presentation with this: Earlier in my career, as a psychologist at the county jail, I had an experience that brought my professional practice to the edge of an understanding of crisis and hostage negotiations. My duties and responsibilities included the assessment and short-term treatment of pretrial detainees, misdemeanants serving time, and convicted felons awaiting transfer to state prison. The welfare, health and safety of inmates, staff, and the security of the institution and the public, and the preservation of property constituted my daily concerns; it entailed seeing most new inmates, particularly those with mental health or substance abuse problems (most inmates!) and following-up on those seen previously. I was ethically bound to treat everyone without regard to their charges and without discrimination; they were my "patients."

An 18-year-old manchild, undernourished, acne marked, and, by all appearances, of low intelligence and educational attainment (high school dropout) was referred to me for evaluation of his risk for suicide. He was charged with the rape of a six-month-old – a shocking crime that involved the penetration of this female infant. He had been asked by the child's mother, a neighbor, to babysit, as he was always available – an inadequate adolescent who had no friends and no social skills or outlets; he was by himself on that weekend night. He watched television as he smoked pot. The baby woke from sleep fitfully and cried. He tried to quiet the fretful infant by dandling her on his lap. The wet diaper, the warmth, and the pressure on his genitals caused a physiological, mechanical event – he got an erection. The disinhibition of the marijuana in this inadequate young man nudged him toward the sexual abuse of someone so vulnerable. A horrific crime for reasons well understood by my audiences. It pained me in what then was the worst criminal violation I had ever heard or imagined. It was the first but by no means the last time I would be horrified by something one of my "patients" had done.

I realized that if I were to judge him and let my repulsion and anger at his predation become known, I would not be able to have influence on him in a helpful therapeutic way, something I had to do ethically; to allow my feelings to be known would kill any possible rapport. Without a minimum of rapport, I could not effectively assess and treat him. I simply had to suspend my judgment and control my true feelings lest they leak out. I found that I could do so by reframing and recasting the Subject as a person in crisis – not such a stretch. He was indeed in crisis twice over; once, as a pathetic, isolated, social misfit without a future, and, again, as an incarcerated sexual offender, about to face the tough consequences of his actions in the criminal justice and correctional systems. Never mind that he had brought it about himself and had needlessly harmed a child, her parents, and countless others. He had to be seen as a person, a human being, in crisis in order to be treated; punishment would come later and from elsewhere. It is this, the central organizing principle of crisis negotiations that I propose as the means to resolve critical incidents and the thesis of *Crisis Negotiation for Law Enforcement, Corrections, and Emergency Services.* The Subject is a person in crisis who, for a brief time at least, must be treated as such without regard for his odious acts.

Crisis negotiations views the Subject as a person in crisis even if it is of his doing and without regard for his antisocial behavior leading up to and during the crisis incident. By "without regard," I do not mean so literally. I do not mean that his or her acts are excused or not taken into account, but that Negotiators suspend their judgment and guide their strategic actions accordingly for the duration of the incident in order to aid the development of the rapport and to facilitate a resolution of the incident. To do otherwise may risk a Negotiator's effective use of self and his ability to influence the Subject – it may come at the cost of a resolution, life and limb. To see the Subject as a person in crisis, rather than as a perpetrator (though in some events he/she may well be one in the same), allows for an empathic rapport that is the key to resolution and the safety of all concerned and the public at large. While it can be difficult to empathize with a "bad actor," reframing the incident as a projection of that actor's internal and external conflicts better fits a "quasi-treatment," negotiation situation. That reframe feeds the Subject's hungry self-centeredness and shifts the focus to his underlying needs and feelings; the focus on underlying needs and concerns is the quasi-treatment that can foster a short-term resolution to the current dangerous situation. The Subject's dilemma (hostage taking, barricade, high-profile suicide threatening) is the current incident in play, and they and their dilemma are seen as negotiable entities.

As a student of hostage negotiations for over 28 years, I cannot recall a single instructor ever acknowledging that mental health professionals (MHP) brought order, structure, and sound principles to what was a ragged police response that almost guaranteed someone would get seriously injured or die – police officers, Subjects, bystanders. A MPH, namely Dr. Harvey Schlossberg of the NYPD, developed the very field itself as he cobbled together psychological principles, widely accepted at the time, to create a discipline – the field of hostage negotiations; its principles and practices are universal and still inform us nearly 40 years later.

Crisis negotiations has come to supplant the narrower construct of hostage negotiations. Law enforcement agencies increasingly found that what they faced daily were more general crisis situations other than ones that involved the taking of hostages, e.g., escalated domestic calls, barricaded Subjects, high-risk warrants, school shootings, and high-profile suicide threats, etc. *Crisis negotiation* is an adaptation of *crisis intervention*, a short-term, mental health emergency treatment as practiced by mental health professionals and disaster relief workers. Most police *Crisis* Negotiators (*hostage* negotiators) do not know the debt owed to the field of crisis intervention. Why is that important? It is important because it grounds the field in its larger context – a means of dealing with the crises of others, people in *extremis* that become public safety concerns. As a field, it offers a structure that is a template of good, sound, principles and practices, proven effective in numerous and varied situations for the nontactical management of those whose acts evidence their personal crises, and, who, in many cases endanger others and the safety and security of the public.

Crisis intervention and crisis negotiations are not exactly the same thing, but because the one derives from the other, they are very similar and are compatible cross-pollinators – each instructs the other. *Crisis* Negotiators benefit from an understanding of what crisis interveners do, why they do what they do, and how they do it. Much of what they do and how they do it is directly applicable to crisis negotiations. How the two differ will be discussed in the following chapter.

My intention here is to: introduce *Crisis* Negotiators to their roots in crisis intervention; provide a structure and framework for conducting negotiations, and illumine the specifics of conducting crisis negotiations within a crisis intervention framework. It is my hope that by doing this I will have increased the breadth and depth of understanding that Negotiators can employ in enhancing their skills and increasing their effectiveness to the benefit of those they serve. While presented in a step-by-step fashion, it is not meant to followed rigidly – flexibility, guidance, deliberateness, adaptation, and good fit are the operative words. I have employed Roberts (2005) seven-stage model of crisis intervention as an illustrative framework, as follows: Stage I – Establish Rapport and Collaborative Relationship; Stage II – Plan and Conduct Biopsychosocial Assessment and Including Lethality; Stage III – Identify Dimensions of Presenting Problem; Stage IV – Explore Feelings and Emotions; Stage V – Generate and Explore Alternatives; Stage VI – Develop and Formulate an Action Plan; and Stage VII – Follow-Up.

In this book, as in the previous ones, I have used the convention of capitalizing the titles, "Subject" and "Negotiator" so that they might stand out more clearly in the text. Different gender pronouns have been used casually as much for variety as anything. Where you see "him" or "her," you may interchange the two as you choose. Negotiators and Subjects come in both genders. As this book has been written as the third part of a trilogy, the reader is urged to read the other two, as well (they need not be read in any strict order): *Communication in Crisis and Hostage Negotiations*, and *Training Strategies for Crisis and Hostage Negotiations*.

Chapter 1

NEGOTIATION AS CRISIS INTERVENTION, CRISIS INTERVENTION AS NEGOTIATION

The principles and goals of crisis negotiation and crisis intervention merge substantially. Crisis intervention and crisis negotiations are not separate entities; they inform each other. Negotiators can and do intervene, and use their skills in a variety of crisis situations that do not involve hostages or barricaded Subjects. They are crises in that they are driven by the "disequilibrium" from within an individual which they act out because their impaired thinking has led them to choose maladaptive ways – that has made things worse for them, and has brought their situation into the public and the attention of the authorities. Only some 18% of critical incidents involve hostages; 82% of the remaining incidents are nevertheless police matters where negotiation teams can react and respond with their considerable negotiation skills. Non-hostage situations that law enforcement and correctional personnel might respond to: *barricaded* Subject, high-risk suicide attempt, domestic violence, prison or jail disturbances, mental health warrants, high-risk felony warrants, violence in public places (workplace, schools), and critical incident stress debriefings (CISD) (McMains & Mullins, 1996).

CRISIS INTERVENTION

Crisis intervention is a "form of brief psychotherapy that emphasizes identification of the specific event precipitating the emotional trauma and uses methods to neutralize that trauma (APA, 1994)." "It is an urgent and acute psychological intervention characterized by immediacy, proximity, expectancy, and brevity." The goals for CI are: (1) *stabilization* – to stop the victim's (Subject's) escalating distress; (2) *mitigating* – to make the Subject's acute signs (symptoms that can be observed by others) and symptoms (experienced and reported by Subject) less severe or painful; (3) to *restore adaptive independent functioning*, if possible, or facilitate access to a higher level of care, i.e., hospitalization (Flannery & Everly, 2000, p. 120). In the present context, an individual or team, invited or uninvited, is introduced into an on-going critical incident to engage a Subject acting out their personal drama publicly. The Subject may welcome the intervener's presence as an answer to his "cry for help" – stop me before I do something terrible to myself or someone else – or the opposite; they may angrily oppose the imposition and interruption. If the Subject has acted out very publicly, the intervener is more likely to be a law enforcement official – a police or corrections officer or specially trained firefighter, EMT, ER medical practitioner (MD, RN), or mental health professional.

Roberts and Ottens (2005) insist that crisis intervention must be voluntary, delivered quickly, and on an as-needed basis. They correctly acknowledge the subjectivity of crisis: "A crisis is personal and is dependent on the individual's perception of the potentially crisis-inducing event their personality and temperament, life experiences and varying degrees coping skills." The core crisis is from within the self. Roberts and Dziegielewski (1995) proffer that "a crisis event can provide an opportunity, a challenge to life goals, a rapid deterioration of functioning or a positive turning point in the quality of one's life." It can go one way or the other. The two Chinese (Japanese) characters for the word "crisis" have been translated as "danger and opportunity" (Green, Lee, Trask, & Rheinscheld, as cited in Dass-Brailsford, 2007) – a paradox that describes an "it can go either way" outcome.

Crisis Intervention is at its essence an emergency psychosocial treatment modality; nonmental health professionals (MHP) occupying that role are acting in the capacity of quasi-therapists (resembling) who have been specially trained by MHP, and may be supported by them in the field (see Slatkin, 2000).

Where a person, by his or her current actions, has threatened or acted in ways that place theirs or the lives of others at serious risk, they may become the Subject of a law enforcement critical incident, an event that impacts on the safety or security of an individual or the public at large. Law enforcement's response focus will be to engage the

Subject (intervene) and negotiate with him in order to resolve the crisis in the interests of public safety and security. Historically, police response, in the days before hostage negotiations emerged as an alternative strategy, was a bold use of force (tactical entry) – kicking the door down; someone was invariably injured or killed; that somebody might have included the Subject, innocent hostages and bystanders, and, frequently, entry team officers by misfire, misadventure, or a provoked Subject. Hostage negotiations, devised as a response to hostage taking and airline hijacking that spiked in the 1960–1970s, was the first orderly use of crisis intervention and negotiations as a deliberate police strategy and tactic.

Historically, most crisis intervention response was directed at recognizable victims of trauma, e.g., survivors suffering serious physical and/or psychological stress (Dass-Brailsford, p. 94); some examples of crises:

- Accident (automotive, airplane, train, explosion, industrial)
- Death, loss of loved one (serious injury or death of family, friends, or others in a shared event)
- Natural disaster (earthquakes, volcanic eruptions, tornadoes, mudslides, floods)
- Physical illness (acute serious, chronic and/or terminal)
- Divorce/separation, marital discord (conflictual human relationships)
- Unemployment (loss of income, benefits, and status)
- Financial difficulties (indebtedness, foreclosure, bankruptcy)

The definition of "victim" has been expanded. To these we add serial military deployments (family separation) and war trauma (PTSD, TBI, and other disabling wounds), refugee status, crime victimhood; alcohol or drug addiction, torture survivors, work strain, etc. In our context, we can add the crises of involvement in: barricade situations, high-risk suicide attempts, domestic violence, prison or jail disturbances, mental health warrants, high-risk felony warrants, violence in public places (workplace, schools), critical incident stress debriefings (CISD), acts of terror, kidnappings, and hostage taking. It may be a stretch for some to include normal people temporarily overwhelmed by stress, hostage takers, criminals caught unawares, and barricaded Subjects. The list of stressors is endless – all may be "an upset in the steady state" (Roberts & Ottens, 2005) – and, any may precipitate "disequilibrium," trauma, and finally reach the level of crisis. Whether or not that happens depends upon many factors within the individual, their relationships, and their environment – their biopsychosocial self.

Characteristics of Crisis Event [Caplan, as cited in Roberts & Ottens (2005)]:
- The precipitating event is perceived as threatening (to the self – physically or psychologically);
- There is an apparent inability to alter or reduce the impact of the event (coping methods are ineffectual) and daily living is disrupted;
- There is increased fear, tension, and/or confusion (it escalates, anxiety and depression increase);
- There is a high level of subjective discomfort (distress increases and the person feels overwhelmed, panicky);
- A state of disequilibrium is followed by rapid transition to an active state of crisis (failure to resolve the crisis may result in psychological breakdown or "mental collapse"). Things get bad, things get worse, things get terrible!

On the *Basic Principles of Crisis Intervention* a number of researchers have come up with three factors they consider very important agents of change: (1) *ventilation and abreaction* (emotional release), (2) *social support*, and (3) *adaptive coping* (Flannery & Everly, 2000, p.120). Additional principles include: *immediate intervention; stabilization; facilitation of understanding; focus on problem solving; encouragement of self-reliance* (Flannery & Everly, 2000, p. 120). The compatibility, even overlapping and sameness, of these principles with a crisis negotiation is clear.

Crises can be characterized as occurring in stages – a logical and linear construct – the first is *Precrisis*, followed by *Crisis, Accommodation/Negotiation*, and finally, *Resolution* (McMains & Mullins, 1994, pp. 42–46). Caplan (as cited in Roberts & Ottens, 2005) delineates four stages of crisis reaction in the individual: (1) initial rise in tension occurs in response to an event; (2) increased tension disrupts daily living; (3) unresolved tension results in depression; and (4) failure to resolve the crisis may result in a psychological breakdown. Roberts sees the intervention as a staged process as well.

Roberts' Seven-Stage Crisis Intervention Model

Roberts' Seven-Stage Crisis Intervention Model (R-SSCIM) (Roberts, 1991, 1995, 1998, 2005) presents a road map for crisis responding that will be used here as the basis for a fuller explication of crisis intervention as crisis negotiation (crisis negotiation as crisis intervention) in the ensuing chapters.

Roberts proffers seven stages which he calls "essential, sequential, and sometimes overlapping" in the crisis intervention process:

I. Plan and conduct a thorough assessment to include a biopsychosocial history and a lethality/imminent dangerousness measure;
II. Make psychological contact and rapidly establish the collaborative relationship;
III. Identify the major problems, including crisis precipitants;
IV. Encourage an exploration of feelings and emotions;
V. Generate and explore alternatives and new coping strategies;
VI. Restore functioning through implementation of an action plan;
VII. Plan follow-up and booster sessions.

Roberts' order has been changed slightly, that is, Stages I and II have been reversed. Placing rapport before assessment makes more sense because it is the basis on which a Negotiator can ask assessment-like questions and expect answers; some relationship, however tentative, should be present before a Negotiator probes deeper and a Subject can consider answering; in the absence of a rapport, a Subject might well answer, "What's it any of your f------ business?"

While establishing rapport, a more free-wheeling process, information is likely to be revealed that meets assessment goals as well – a least intrusive way of getting needed information initially. As the rapport develops, follow-on and more direct queries may be made. While assessment is critical to planning and, ultimately to a safe outcome, a collaborative relationship must be sought as it is the basis for any helping relationship – both parties need to feel that they have a stake in dialoguing – that something "might could come of it" in the interests, as yet undefined, of both. And so, rapport precedes assessment although they are more practically, and realistically, effected simultaneously. Answers to assessment queries not asked may be revealed spontaneously. Practically speaking, rapport building and assessment happen coincidently.

Crisis intervention is just that – an attempt to step between (intervene/interrupt) an individual and his or her crisis so as to mediate further actions in their stuck state. That it is a crisis implies that there are potentially serious consequences, including but not exclusively loss of life, if the individual is left on his or her own (not intervened on). It is a type of psychological treatment with a set of principles and practices that have been field-tested over more than 50 years in a variety of emergent and critical situations. While crisis intervention may be plied in the office of a physician or mental health practitioner, emergency room, a hotline, or ER, it is frequently played out in public venues where the police are called upon to intervene, for example, a "jumper" on a heavily-trafficked local bridge.

As so many crises have played out in public, with public safety and security as prominent concerns, crisis intervention has become the responsibility, no, the legal mandate of police departments (failure to act, ineffectual performance, failure to train are potential liabilities), in particular. HNTs, once confined to hostage and barricade situations, were under-utilized. They were often not called out to respond to a critical incident because it did not involve a hostage taking or barricaded Subject. In the late 1990s, the FBI changed its bureau designator on HNT (Hostage Negotiation Team) to Crisis Negotiation Unit (CNU) to take into account the wider scope and increasing frequency of incidents that involved an individual in crisis but that did not involve the taking of hostages. Nonhostage incidents, particularly escalated domestic abuse incidents, had long since supplanted those involving the taking of hostages in frequency of occurrence. The techniques that hostage negotiators employed were practical and well suited for dealing with crises in addition to and other than those in which a third party was being held against his or her will, as a bargaining chip in demands of the police, or a reluctant and *barricaded* Subject (metaphorically holding him/herself hostage). Many departments have changed unit designators and missions from HNT to CNT; still others have added specially trained Crisis Intervention Teams (CIT). The majority have embraced a wider role ("mission creep") for Negotiators that intervene in critical incidents in play and negotiate a safe and secure outcome (resolution).

Regardless of the type of crisis event, the focus is on the Subject (the principal actor, perpetrator, threatener). While the crisis event is of their doing – it is the Subject's personal crisis (internal/external) that has been projected onto the world – the crisis that led to the crisis. Projection means the shining of one's inner perceptions, thoughts, and feelings onto the world (like a movie projector shines the film image onto a screen) and then misperceives what he sees or feels as reality, failing to identify the origin as his own inner life shown on the screen.

Hostage Negotiations as Crisis Intervention and Negotiation

Crisis negotiation has as its focus the Subject, the individual at the center of the crisis. In keeping with the central organizing principle proposed here, this includes what would not have been construed as a crisis warranting an intervention unless that intervention were a tactical police response, a hostage taking or *barricaded* Subject incident; however, hostage takers and *barricaded* Subjects generally meet the criteria for individuals in crisis while, at the same time, they also create crises for others. At first, their acts may be written off as simply criminal or crazy, the crisis being a consequence of the Subject's own doing: a deliberate criminal act or misadventure, unrestrained domestic violence, impaired judgment by a destabilized, distraught or impaired individual, the irrational thinking of an emotionally or mentally disordered person or a maladaptive attempt by a normal person to cope with overwhelming stress. Regardless, the Subject can be seen as a person in crisis (with a little stretch) despite his opprobrium, stupidity, or irrationality. An incident where a perpetrator is seen as "dumb" or is written off as "crazy" or a "dirtbag" cannot be effectively negotiated. While it may rankle some to think of a perpetrator as a person in crisis (or worse still, a victim), it is useful, for our purposes to do so. A perpetrator in crisis can be negotiated with. Negotiation as crisis intervention is the framework, a structured, orderly, and effective means of approaching, influencing, and facilitating a person in crisis to "do the right thing."

"Bad actors" – criminal perpetrators – are callous, self-centered, unempathic, sociopathic, antisocial, authority-baiting persons who victimize others without regard for their health and safety. They are not likeable! If the goal and objective is a safe resolution, then it must be realized that to see the Subject only in terms of his or her unacceptable and more repellant behaviors and character traits, and to respond to them, thinking and feeling about them in that way (mindset), will likely preclude the development of a rapport; such attitudes and mindset on the part of a Negotiator will leak out even if disguised or suppressed – it will show through. If it does, then it will exacerbate the problem and lead to a contentious and combustible encounter – the opposite of a rapport; again, rapport is the foundation on which the negotiations rest – without it, the Negotiator will not be accepted nor heard nor will his or her influence be felt, and negotiation goals will not be met.

A *crisis* Negotiator must learn to *suspend judgment*, for at least as long as the incident's duration, not simply cover over nor pretend to not feel one way or to feel another. In order to get to a place of suspended judgment, a Negotiator must *reframe* the hostage taker or barricaded Subject as a person in crisis; in this way, the Negotiator enables himself/herself to see the Subject as "in crisis" and therefore as someone in need. Most can relate to having a problem they cannot solve (it exceeds a person's ability to cope at the time) and the sometimes absurd reasoning that can surface in the struggle to cope and maintain equilibrium. Meeting the Subject's needs is accomplished through negotiation, and because the Subject is at the center of it, he is the key to resolving the incident. A person in crisis can be worked with – their needs and vulnerabilities are made apparent through their original actions and all that follows over the course of the negotiations (what they do and say).

Reframing allows for a focus on the Subject in a way that sets aside the repellent parts in the interest of a safe resolution. Also, it has a coherent, orderly, and proven-effective means of structuring an intervention that is a blend of crisis intervention and police negotiation=CRISIS NEGOTIATION. There are other means of getting to a compassionate, quasi-therapeutic negotiation stance which may be found within the individual *crisis* Negotiator, e.g., religious creed, humanism.

Even a "true believer," a religious or political zealot or cult member – a Subject driven by a fanatical belief – can be reframed as in crisis; the standoff with police is indeed a crisis, but the inner turmoil that the Subject faces is made up of the intense emotions that brought him to his beliefs: ambivalent feelings, confused and contradictory thoughts and ideas, and dueling confidence and certainty versus nagging doubt. The Subject is human, although his acts may have been unspeakable and inhumane, and so, he brings to his beliefs the life experiences that shaped him and formed his personality; he did not choose his group affiliation randomly or lightly nor the role he would play; he could have joined another, less violent group or opted to be on the sidelines or in the background. His choices are his projections onto the world – he has "issues," and, thus vulnerabilities, e.g., anger, depression, self-righteousness, resentment, losses, grievances, etc., Subjects are motivated (driven) by their underlying psychic issues. Their "cause" is one way they channel their needs and their dysfunctional self, and Negotiators may access that inner self through the Subject-Negotiator encounter. See them as in crisis, treat them as if in crisis, and find the road to resolution by addressing their crisis.

Hostage takings, barricade situations, and other incidents law enforcement personnel are likely to respond to are crises for law enforcement and public safety; however, they are not traditionally thought of as crisis situations with respect to the Subjects (perpetrators) themselves. It is easy to see a Subject threatening suicide as in the throes of a personal crisis, not so for the terrorist hostage taker. A hostage taker has committed an act that may be coldly calculating or desperate. In either case, the hostage taker is at the center of the incident and is subject to the same stresses and strains of any person in crisis; he or she has strengths and weaknesses of character and commitment, and mental constructs (feeling, thinking) as does anyone else. If we construe the Subject as in crisis – what he is doing is what he (the Subject) chose to do – one that reflects his state of mind. Terrorist hostage taking, for example, calls for a power struggle with the authorities in which the hostage taker tries to exploit his captives for some gain. He must negotiate with the police by definition; hostage taking is about leveraging his position for some gain. But, again, he too has not lived his life in a vacuum and his issues, internal and external, informed those choices. Why not (subtlely) shift the focus more onto the Subject (a wedge), as a person in crisis, rather than wholly on the incident? For a Subject in crisis we have at our disposal the whole methodology of crisis negotiations delivered through crisis intervention.

By creating an incident, a Subject has exposed himself to the negotiation process and a Negotiator's influence. He is in a position that pits his aims against those of the public; he needs to get us (the authorities) out of his way – we are interfering with his plans, or alternatively, to get something he wants or needs – he must go through us.

To reiterate, a Subject in crisis can be "treated" (to a greater or lesser degree) in a quasi-therapeutic manner as the goals of crisis intervention and negotiations overlap in significant ways in many areas, e.g., some but not all strategies, stratagems, tactics, and techniques are common to crisis intervention and crisis negotiations. What is called for here is an extension of this construct to other less traditional crisis Subjects. *Crisis* Negotiators need to be grounded in the crisis intervention/negotiations model to do so.

Differences in Crisis Intervention and Crisis Negotiation

Some differences between hostage negotiations and crisis intervention as practiced by a mental health professionals (MHP) are bound up in the requirements of ethical standards, some of which are also legal requirements. Potential ethical conflicts: lying, exploitation (instrument of police tactical action), e.g., stalling subject while police seek tactical advantage and/or sniper shot.

MHP make referrals for specialized or continued treatment and other follow-up as appropriate as their goals and objectives are therapeutic, that is, they are directed at change, growth, amelioration of symptoms, and the development of new coping skills. Crisis negotiators may have even more pressing legal strictures and liabilities and face greater public scrutiny.

Most *crisis interveners* and negotiators are not MHP; both could benefit from the presence, monitoring, and support of a postgraduate trained MHP on the team.

SUMMARY

Crisis intervention is crisis negotiation is crisis intervention. There is a convergence of the two. The goals and principles of both are nearly identical and substantially compatible and complementary, enough so that it is a "distinction without a difference." Crisis intervention (CI) can be seen as the framework for its means and the means for the practice of crisis negotiation (CN). When all Subjects are seen as "in crisis" they and the incidents they have created make them negotiable. Where crisis interveners "facilitate," crisis negotiators "negotiate." Where crisis interveners negotiate, crisis negotiators facilitate. Each does both as appropriate.

CI and CN focus on the intense emotions that characterize crisis incidents and Subjects in crisis. Goals for both include: ventilation of feelings, movement to and through problem solving, and planning and resolution; the amelioration of distress and the mitigation of crisis' effects, too, are central to what each aims at.

Chapter 2

STAGE I: RAPIDLY ESTABLISH RAPPORT AND A COLLABORATIVE RELATIONSHIP

> A young bride-to-be described the qualities she loved in her intended, something she considered a rarity of rarities among men, "He knew how to listen and asked questions in a very sensitive way."
>
> Copage (July 29, 2012)

Objective: "Establish rapport and rapidly establish collaborative relationship" (Roberts & Ottens, 2005).

The initial phase of crisis negotiations, like that of any therapeutic, business or social relationship, requires the parties to "break the ice." Introductions are made and the parties look to find some common interest. First impressions are based partially (largely?) on how each is perceived by the other. How each is perceived by the other is based partially (largely?) on how well each is willing to listen to the other and to reveal something of themselves.

The establishment of a relationship, a connection, a rapport is the basis for what is to follow. If you cannot make a connection with someone, then how can you expect to bargain with them? The rapport in negotiations is about convincing, even if just tentatively, the other that you are willing to listen and will be respectful, i.e., not dismissing or discounting him. By listening and being respectful, you acknowledge the Subject – no one wants to feel invisible or be put down. For the Subject, it may be no small matter as he or she may have little ego-strength, a long history of rejection or failure and self-loathing – someone who has not found anyone willing to listen – to acknowledge him or her. It may not be easy to connect with someone whose behavior leading up to the incident and during the incident that the Negotiator, and most everybody else, finds ugly. Nonetheless, a way must be found. Listening is the means to a rapport; it is the rapport.

Effective communication is at the crux of hostage negotiations, especially, though not exclusively, in the crucial task of establishing *rapport.* It is crucial here because it is the initial contact between Negotiator and Subject ("first impressions" and "getting off on the right foot") – it sets the tone and tenor for the negotiations. It is the foundation on which all that follows rests.

RAPPORT

Rapport is an essential ingredient in all relationships and the hostage taker-Negotiator relationship is no exception. Before any meaningful negotiations can take place, a bridge or bond of some kind must be established. Like and trust may be a part of that connection, however cautious and tentative, shallow, and short-lived. A collaborative connection of some kind must be perceived – like it or not we're in this together. Ultimately, Negotiator and hostage taker – for better or for worse – are married – their fates are joined. The objective of negotiations is to resolve the crisis and the means is that of a "collaborative relationship" negotiating the details and terms. And so, hostage taker and Negotiator seek a face-saving resolution that works for all.

Fair market value is a business concept that holds, a fair price for something is one to which both buyer and seller agree, even if each has given up some of what they wanted (and gotten only some of what they wanted). This has some relevance here in that the collaborative relationship between Negotiator and Subject, and by means of negotiations, produces a resolution that all parties can accept even if somewhat begrudgingly. While the underlying problem, e.g., chronic depression, job loss, impending incarceration, etc., will go unresolved, the immediate public crisis may be resolved allowing for more lasting solutions, e.g., substance abuse counseling, to come later and in a different venue.

In a collaborative relationship, the Negotiator steers the "conversation" while "hooking" the Subject in a way that leads them to a deal – it entails a receptive listener and a persuasive speaker. (Again, receptiveness is mediated by rapport.) Everyone is ambivalent about their feelings – those feelings in particular that lead people into such public crises as suicide in front of an audience. Ambivalence, or mixed and often contradictory feelings occurring simultaneously, allows the Negotiator to tilt the Subject towards a decision favoring safety, stability, and eventual resolution. In referring to a jumper on a bridge, an officer has the goal to form a rapport with the Subject and "seize upon the one emotional chord . . . that will get him or her to climb down from the edge" (Ruderman, 2012).

Rapport, from the seventeenth century French, is defined as a "relationship, *especially* a relationship characterized by harmonious accord. A . . . state of deep spiritual, emotional, or mental connection between people." The American Psychological Association's definition – its therapeutic usage – adds: a "mutual responsiveness that contributes to the patient's confidence in the therapist and willingness to work cooperatively." To put it simply, a rapport is a positive, collaborative connection that is formed between parties. Some connections are instantaneous ("love at first sight") while most take some working at, indicating that both conscious and subconscious factors are at play.

Instant like or dislike notwithstanding, rapport can be built in most cases, if not by one Negotiator, then by another. The psychopath may be an exception. A barricaded Subject may voice his bias, "I can't talk to a woman," another might say, in a bid for control, "I won't talk to you. Put someone else on the phone." However, in the end, the principal ingredient may be largely the form rather than the substance (content) of the rapport–building dance and dialogue. The Negotiator's, demonstrated patience, respect, willingness to listen, suspension of judgment, and persistence may win out over, for example, similarities between Negotiator and Hostage Taker such as gender, shared religious heritage, or life experiences. (Career criminals, like psychopaths, may not be able to truly connect with anyone, but they may do so conditionally, on a shallow, pragmatic, self-interested basis, "You're my ticket out of here.") The formation of the bond is aided by the Negotiator's mien, even if it is scoffed at by the Subject contemptuously. In all cases, the Negotiator is tested to see if she or he is "worthy" and willing to persist at it despite the open abuse or passive resistance.

Where rapport *is not* instantaneous, or easily achieved, and building is required, there are some principles and techniques that have proved helpful in promoting its development. Where rapport *is* instantaneous or easily achieved, those same principles and techniques fix and maintain a rapport that might otherwise deteriorate for one reason or another.

Some of those principles are: Respectful engagement, tolerance, a nonjudgmental set, perceived acknowledgement and acceptance, placidity, encouragement and reinforcement, empathy, and effective communication, especially *active listening*. The principles are a combination of a Negotiator's personal qualities and professional skills.

Respectful Engagement

A "display of respect" can usually be seen as transparently phony and insincere. The use of predicates such as "sir" are usually a tip off to a scripted response that does not ring true (Police officers are notorious for referring to a serial murderer in custody or being sought as the "gentleman)." Something approaching a sincere, respectful manner, even if only situational and of short duration, needs to be called up.

Respect can be general – for the person as a human being however flawed ("We are all God's creatures") – or particular (a combat veteran like myself). Despite a Negotiator's radically different value system, even a strong revulsion for the Subject's lifestyle or criminal acts, he or she must compartmentalize those thoughts and feelings about the Subject and find a way through them in the moment. Regardless, some kernel of respect, however conditional, must be found for the Negotiator to set the tone that engenders mutual regard – the rapport. Respect is communicated by tone, manner, choice of words, and acknowledgement – what we communicate and how we communicate it. A Negotiator must find within himself a note of respect and convey it to the Subject by their manner ("I am sickened by this woman and what she has done to her children, but I understand that the things she has experienced in life must have been horrific. That is not to excuse her or mitigate the criminality of her act or discount the victimhood of the innocent child."); "People like her, so damaged, and with so little going for them – it's pathetic – but human at its most primitive. There but for the grace. . . .").

The engagement part refers to the means and manner and is conveyed by and through the cited principles made up of personal qualities and professional skills.

Engagement: Tolerance, Acceptance, Suspension of Judgment, and Empathy

It is a challenge to be tolerant and accepting of someone whose values, lifestyle or frank criminality is inimical and repugnant to the Negotiator. The Negotiator is challenged to suspend judgment for the period that includes the duration of the negotiations and the resolution of the incident. How do you begin to *tolerate, accept,* and *suspend your judgment* of someone who has raped and murdered a child, the reported crime that led to the police attempt to execute a warrant and precipitated the alleged perpetrator's present standoff? To not do so is to risk the rapport that is necessary to negotiate and that may avert further loss of life or injury. To not do so is to limit law enforcement's options to only tactical ones.

Tactical options may be the eventual and inevitable choice in the end, but to not attempt to negotiate in good faith is a legal liability that could be costly. Additionally, tactical operations increase the likelihood of injury or fatalities to officers, hostages, bystanders, and hostage takers.

It is helpful to "compartmentalize" the Subject's distasteful characteristics and reprehensible actions, that is, to separate and isolate them in a separate "compartment." Keep what they are and what they did that is alien to you, the Negotiator, and negotiate with the remaining part – the person apart from the monster. Consider the sports hero, whom we fan-worship who, it turns out, beats his wife after each game, or in corollary fashion, the armed robber who volunteers at the "Y" with troubled youth. Human beings are complicated and complex. One more example: A soldier denigrates and dehumanizes his enemy as a "gook" or a "raghead" – a sub-human – so that he can bring himself to kill him. He hates the enemy that has shot at him and has killed his comrades. After the battle, a soldier searches the corpse of an enemy soldier, and his personal effects, for anything of intelligence value. Going through the dead man's wallet, a photograph of the man with his family is found – the enemy soldier's family is like his own, a wife and three children about the same age as his own kids. Letters from home found in his helmet lining reveal that he was a conscript and that he was the same age; he had planned to finish college after the war, same as the surviving soldier. A common humanity is revealed.

Regardless of whether it is rooted in religion or secularism, a Negotiator may connect with a Subject's humanity as a flawed human being in trouble for lots of reasons, including his own bad choices. It is through *empathy*, the ability to step into another's world, see it through their eyes, and understand them and their dilemma. "There but for the grace. . . ."

Some Helpful Negotiator Qualities

Some Negotiator qualities and traits are inborn or learned early on in the home environment. Parents and siblings reinforce them and friends choose them because of those very reasons. Negotiators self-select; that is, those with helpful qualities and traits of character and behavior are most often the ones who apply to be on the HNT, and are selected for the team by the interview panel. Some qualities and behaviors, however, can be learned, practiced, and developed. Below are some qualities and behaviors that are thought to be helpful for Negotiators.

Flexibility and Resiliency – the ability to adapt to or bounce back from a surprising or changing situation or a unique Subject. While the crisis intervention model is orderly, a Subject or the situation might very well mix-up the expected order, one or more times; being able to meet the individual where s/he is or where the incident "is" without trying to force him or "it" into a mold suggested by the model or the Negotiator's expectations – sometimes the incident begins at Stage IV or V and circles back to I and back to V again. Plans are not reality and may have to be tweaked or even scrapped; a Negotiator cannot be rigidly wed to a plan that is, after all, just projection into an uncertain future.

Aplomb – is a confident, self-assured, and poised response in the face of challenges, reversals, abusive language, changing and off-balancing happenings, etc., without being thrown. Being asked an embarrassing question that you would rather not answer and are not sure how you should answer calls for aplomb. Responding in a matter-of-factly manner, without visible anger or frustration, to a hostage taker's up-ante demands is aplomb.

Creativity – is a valuable tool in a Negotiator's toolbox. It is a means of dealing with unique situations and individuals, or even common situations, in new ways. It is the medium through which *flexibility* is made manifest. Using active listening techniques like recipes makes the Negotiator's responses sound canned or scripted. Negotiator's need to find their own voice and ways of relating that fits them and the unique individual they are encountering. It reaches deeper to find what might work.

Healthy Sense of Self/Good Ego Strength – "know thy self" – is a good starting point for anyone entering any kind of relationship. It ensures greater honesty, sincerity, flexibility, resiliency, creativity, appropriate boundaries, *self-confidence*, clearer thinking and judgment, and freedom from bias. It is this quality that underpins and encompasses all of the others.

Genuineness – being comfortable with oneself allows for a genuine or authentic way of relating – a way that is not ego driven, inflated, phony, or self-congratulatory. Sincerity and self-trust allow a Negotiator to be himself/herself; it is a "technique-less" way of relating that eschews "playing the Negotiator role."

Self-Confidence – stems from a realistic self-appraisal, self-knowledge, and knowledge of the discipline of hostage negotiations; skills learned, developed, practiced, and tested in the real world give a Negotiator the confidence to master herself/himself and the intricacies of crisis intervention/hostage negotiations.

A Positive Attitude – does not mean a phony show of high spirits – a painted-on smile, but, rather, a realistic outlook, neither overly pessimistic nor overly optimistic – neither extreme is well grounded or helpful. A positive attitude stems from a person's *flexibility and resiliency, genuineness, healthy sense of self/good ego strength, creativity, aplomb,* and *self-confidence.* A positive attitude makes for realistic expectations – a hedge against undue frustration, disappointment, and self-blame.

EFFECTIVE COMMUNICATION

Effective communication is too large a topic to deal with here in the detail it would require. Some high points have been selected. The reader is encouraged to follow his or her interests and further his or her research. Principal amongst the communication techniques is *Active Listening.* It will be addressed in some detail below.

Most interventions used in hostage negotiations are verbal encounters by means of the telephone; other verbal interventions not by telephone are not face to face, e.g., through a closed and barricaded door. For this reason, nonverbal techniques are not dealt with here; only selected verbal ones are highlighted.

Voice Quality

Voice quality refers to the use of the vocal organs and apparatus (larynx, vocal cord, tongue, palate, teeth, etc.) and breath – all of which are employed in the production and articulation of sound and speech. Again, there is more to this operation than is possible to cover here and some of which is unnecessary for our purposes. Under *voice quality* we highlight *tone, rate, pitch, volume, intensity, fluency, meter,* and *manner*.

Tone

Tone refers to the quality of a person's voice. Its inflection is expressive of a mood or emotion. In other words, tone conveys the feeling that lies beneath or behind our verbal production. A tone may be angry, forgiving, punitive, loving, kindly, matter-of-factly, condescending, etc. A harsh tone conveys a negative judgment, intolerance, anger, disacknowledgement, etc. The lack of respect or empathy that a negotiator might feel for a Subject may be very apparent or, more subtlely, leak out in his or her tone or manner. If those feelings are detected by the Subject, then he or she will feel disrespected, resentful, and angry, all enemies of trust, mutuality, and rapport ["You think I'm scum, don't you?"(as he hangs up the phone)]. In corollary fashion, a matter-of-fact (neutral) or warm tone can be expected to convey nonjudgment or acceptance; basic rapport-building.

Breath Control

A Subject's emotional state is reflected in their breathing; an anxious person may breathe rapidly and in a pressured way, a depressed person in a slow, labored way. While the emotional state is reflected in a Subject's breathing rate, manner, and depth, it is a reciprocal, that is, altering the rate, manner, and depth can change the Subject's emotional state – an anxious Subject can be stilled by controlling his or her breathing – a technique well known by martial artists and other athletes.

A Negotiator "joins" with an overexcited Subject, first "pacing" him or her and gradually "leading" them to a quieter state by slowing down his/her own breathing; at a subconscious level the Subject is led to breathe "easy" and, by so doing, affect control over his or her excited state.

Pitch, Meter, Rate, Intensity, Fluency, Manner

Other qualities of voice and vocalization that convey the speaker's feelings and meanings include: *Pitch* (the relative vibration frequency or highness/lowness); *meter* (measured or regulated rhythm); *rate* (speed as in fast/slow); *intensity* (loud/soft); and, *fluency* (smoothness or flow). *Manner*, not a quality of speech but rather a way of acting, a bearing or air, is extremely important as well. Similarly, a reading of the Subject's vocalizations (alongside the verbal content), through his or her responses, conveys thoughts and feelings toward the Negotiator and offers valuable feedback about the state of the rapport.

All of the above convey, through our speech presentation, the Negotiator's feelings, and as such may promote or damage rapport. They are part of the whole of our communication that is effective or to the contrary, ineffective, has consequences as the Subject considers, consciously and unconsciously, how we feel and what we think of him. The voice and our speech qualities are all **manipulable**, that is, we may **deliberately** change the rate, and intensity of our speech to create a particular effect. For example, a Negotiator may increase the rate and intensity of his or her speech to stir a sleepy or depressed Subject, or decrease the rate and intensity to calm an agitated Subject.

Loaded Words and Phrases

As with all verbal interventions, care should be taken to be **deliberate** in what is said and done. Deliberate, as used here, means thinking ahead and having in mind a purpose and a desired, sought response or outcome for what you say or do; an important part of this also knowing what not to say. Certain words or phrases may be "loaded" generally or particularly for a given Subject.

It is not possible to "know" all of a Subject's "triggers" or "hot buttons" but, in the course of the negotiations, some of his or her sensitivities may be revealed. Too, informants and historical data from, e.g., arrest records, psychiatric history, etc., may point to possible sensitive areas or toxic Subjects. Some words, are almost universally very risky to use, such as racial epithets. To call someone "stupid" is very risky as most of us would likely take offense; however, there is a proviso here: If we follow the rule of being *deliberate*, we may choose to call someone "stupid" *deliberately* expressly to provoke a particular response in this particular individual, at this particular time. Never say "never."

NLP, Representative Systems, and Mimesis

NLP (Neuro-Linguistic Programming), from communication theory in the 1970–1980s, had a significant impact on the fields of communication, psychotherapy, and hypnosis. One of its most useful understandings is that people express themselves (communicate), at a given time, in one of five "representational systems" (Bandler & Grinder, 1979; Lankton, 1980). Representational systems are sensory channels that correspond to the five senses (visual, auditory, kinesthetic, olfactory, taste), the principal ones are: seeing, hearing, and feeling. Which representative system a person is in, at any given time, can be known by the "predicates" (nouns, verbs, adverbs) they use. For example, a person who says, "I'm trying to *show* you what it's like. Do you *see* where I'm coming from? It couldn't be *clearer*. If you don't *see* it you are *unfocused* or *blind*." Such an exchange can be *clearly viewed* as in the visual representative system. To respond to this Subject in another representative system, other than visual, is to risk having him or her not understand you and feel misunderstood and dis-acknowledged: "I *hear* what you're *saying*. I get it *loud and clear*. It *rings* true too." This auditory-weighted (hearing) response cuts across representative systems and may not register with the Subject as well (effectively) as in his or her expressed system.

Responding to a hostage taker in *his or her* "representative system," by using that system's predicates (matching them), is more likely to register in its content, but, even more importantly, subconsciously, as a rapport bridge that seems to say, "I know you are present. We understand each other. There is a connection here." Rapport.

A similar concept is *mimesis*. As used here, it means using the language of the Subject – his or her words. If a Subject says, "I was stoned," it is better to say, when making reference to a drug-induced state as "stoned" rather than, for example, "wrecked." "Stoned' is the Subject's word for being in a drugged state; "wrecked" is not the Subject's usual term for that state, also it may be "out," placing you, the Negotiator, as an "other." Using the Subject's language – his or her words, terms, and phrase – decreases the perceived divide between you and him or her.

Lying

The question of lying often comes up in regard to crisis and hostage negotiations. Is it permissible to lie? Is it advisable to lie? These questions should be addressed first.

It is arguable whether it is permissible to lie. It used to be taught that you should never lie because you might meet that same Subject again and your credibility (the department's) would be blown. Of course, that is predicated on having been caught in a lie. There is no ethical restraint on lying in hostage negotiations. It is one way that hostage negotiations differ from a therapeutic intervention in which a mental health professional is delivering professional services. Therapists in all of the mental health professions are governed by ethical guidelines; lying might not be specifically prohibited, but it is clearly on the other side of ethical practice. There are no strictures against lying.

Lying should be deliberate and purposeful rather than casual or glib. We may choose to lie to reinforce a Subject's verbalization, to connect with him or her by conveying similarity through self-disclosure ("me too"), to ease their anxiety, influence their thinking or behavior. We do so in the service of promoting negotiation objectives. Lying is permissible, which is different from whether or not it is advisable.

Is it advisable to lie? The risks of lying can be great and serious negative consequences may follow if caught. Recovery may be possible in some few cases, but it violates the desired end of rapport, building trust. If trust is lost, the rapport may be lost, and with it, the effectiveness of the negotiations. That is not to say that it is always a deal breaker, but generally speaking, it should be used deliberately and cautiously. If you choose to lie:

- (the guidelines are taken from practiced and skilled liars) – remember your lies (write them down so that you and those who follow you can be consistent);
- measure future verbalizations against your lies to ensure consistency;
- lie about things you are knowledgeable about;
- stick close to the truth (shading the truth allows you a foundation of truth that is easier to recall and can be better contained);
- if challenged, stick to your story and avoid defensiveness and lengthy defenses or excuses; and,
- the use of "tentative" or "conditional" truths allows for wiggle

room ("To the best of my knowledge . . ." "If everything happens according to plan . . .").

One may lie by either *omission* or *commission* or, as Ekman (1985) proffers, by *concealment* or *falsification*. Lies of omission entail leaving out something on purpose to avoid telling a lie of commission (withholding); not telling the whole truth is a common "way around the truth." Some such lies may have a germ of the truth (not the whole truth) or may "shade" the truth (minimize, spin, color, or reframe it). Lies of commission are deliberate deceits, attempts to misrepresent facts, feelings, and/or intentions (it both withholds what is true and presents what is false as true). In some cases, it may be seen as necessary as in the case of protecting tactical assets and dispositions, e.g., location of snipers. In a special case, a lie might be told as a ploy or manipulation engineered to demonstrate to the Subject that you are joined with him or her in his or her interest (in the interest rapport-building) – "I told the captain that you were cooperating in order to get him to okay sending in the smokes." It should be noted that making promises that you are not be able to keep – because it's out of your control – is to the Subject equivalent to a lie, e.g., "The money you're asking for will be here by noon, guaranteed!"

Some examples of the above (The Subject has shot and killed a coworker before barricading himself in his home):

- He's hurt bad, but it looks like he's going to make it.
- There are guns and there are guns. Because you used a pellet gun they probably won't come down on you as hard.
- People under extreme emotional distress, like you, have made out okay with the courts.
- I'm in a van around the corner, but I never saw any snipers go by.
- There are officers all around the building. That's the truth. (In this case, the negotiator has told the Subject the truth about something he already knows, but that does not compromise the tactical situation). It is a manipulative use of the truth to convince the Subject of your "truthfulness." When a Subject asks a question, you should consider that she may know the answer and is, by her question, testing you.

Whether *lying* or *not lying*, it is recommended that you, the Negotiator, use tentative and conditional language, such as: "probably, best as

I can tell, I can't promise you but . . . , and, it may or may not," if you can get away with it. Telling people what they want to hear goes a long way in getting the Subject to accept what you have said. Hearing what they want to hear is largely, though not completely, a function of the Subject's needs.

Active Listening

Active Listening is a method, a means, a strategy for conveying to another your interest, as a listener, in them and what they have to say. It consists of a number of verbal and nonverbal techniques that, because they are active and demonstrable make clear your engagement ("I hear you and what you are saying"). The object is to convey to the Subject that you are listening, something he or she may have never experienced before from anyone. Being an active listener requires you to pay close attention as well in order to ensure that your responses are accurate and that unclear communications are clarified.

Two major communication errors are in effect the result of the opposite of active listening: *Inattention* and *Premature Assumptions*. *Inattention* is not listening to the other party fully enough as you, the listener, are distracted by your own thoughts and planning your response. *Premature Assumptions* is drawing conclusions based on incomplete, ambiguous, or confusing information. Either or both are likely to be inaccurate and may lead to rapport-killing misunderstandings. They are to be guarded against as they affect both the present dialogue and the greater rapport.

The objectives of active listening can be further understood as a means:

- To build and maintain rapport;
- To slow down or speed up the pace, as called for. A Subject who is speaking too rapidly or volubly may need to be slowed down after a certain point; up to that point, it is "ventilation"; beyond that point it "overload" and has diminishing returns for both the Negotiator and the Subject. For an exhausted, depressed, or characteristically taciturn individual, speeding-up may be a deliberate and called for tactic;
- To convey interest in aid of establishing/maintaining rapport. To the speaker, interest in him and what he has to say is demonstrated by the listener's outright affirmations, acknowledgements, ques-

tions, etc. It feels good to tell your story and know someone is listening. It's easier to like someone who shows interest in you;
- To encourage elaboration of details and other information. Some Subjects may speak sparingly. Asking for detail both conveys interest and prompts the detail that may clarify what has been said and provide information of intelligence value;
- To encourage/discourage the ventilation of overheated emotion or the production of information. Paucity or plenty, too much or too little information or emotion may be counterproductive for the Subject and in aiding the rapport. The Negotiator can deliberately choose whether to encourage or discourage either;
- To give information and direction (correcting misinformation) and making suggestions;
- To seek clarification of a Subject's verbalization that may be vague, confusing, and/or ambiguous;
- To model more open communication; and
- To increase the Subject's perceived identification with the Negotiator.

Active listening says, "I am interested in you and what you are saying; I hear you and I am trying to know what you are saying and what you mean." It is the active, as opposed to a passive listening, that makes the difference. The active part functions as a feedback mechanism; it conveys feedback such as, "Can you be clearer about that?" "I get it." "Tell me more." "I'm having trouble following you."

- The most common and best known of the verbal *active listening* techniques are: *reflection, paraphrasing,* and *minimal encouragers; nonverbal cues,* e.g., where there is face-to-face contact, such as nodding, smiling, etc. are also very effective. There is a risk of sounding scripted and repetitious (rapport-busters) when these techniques are learned and employed in a rote and repeated fashion. Negotiators need to learn a wider variety of techniques and employ them with a deliberate objective each time. Once learned techniques can be "customized" to fit a Negotiator's own style, manner, and personality.

For a fuller treatment of this subject that includes a significantly larger number and greater variety of verbal responses, their specific, intended, deliberate and pointed uses, and expected impact. *Listening, sharing,* and *action* techniques are differentiated, illustrated, and their application made clear; in establishing rapport *listening* and *sharing* responses predominate (see Slatkin, 1995, 2005, 2010).

Generally, it is better to listen more and speak less at this juncture; in later phases, you, the Negotiator, may need to talk more as you offer information to the Subject in exploring options and directing his or her decision to "come out."

Suicide Prevention

If in course of establishing rapport, hints of or overt talk of suicide are revealed then a shift towards a fuller assessment and intervention is called for; it then becomes the first priority. Coincidentally, the time and care taken to explore and support the Subject is a pre-eminent rapport builder. See Chapters 4 and 10 for suicide assessment and intervention.

Use of Humor

Humor is a wonderful human quality and resource. As a tool for connecting with others, it is unsurpassed. Its use in crisis intervention is risky but may be worth it.

The choice to use humor should be guided by the Subject's cues and the Negotiator's tactical decisions and ethical standards: Does the Subject use humor? Is the humor "black humor" (gallows humor)? Is the humor tasteless, degrading, disrespectful to others, or otherwise grossly inappropriate, e.g., promote racial stereotyping (Don't do it!)? From the Negotiator's perspective: Does the use of humor seem inappropriate because of the gravity of the situation? Does the use of humor introduce or add to the degradation of denigration of others? Does the use of humor seem to offer a "handshake," or another way of making a connection? The Negotiator must make a deliberate choice to use humor based of his or her desired objective, gauge the Subject's likely receptiveness and response, and personal/professional ethical considerations, e.g., not to encourage a Subject's extremist and or violent views or hatred of others. Use of humor should always be deliberate, as with any other verbalization.

Humor is very subjective. Some things should not be joked about – its use can be risky but, then again, it is a powerful means of releasing and relieving tension. Self-effacing humor in particular ("This ain't the smartest move I ever made.") is helpful. What one person finds funny may anger another. It leaves a lot of room for misunderstanding, but then so for almost any verbalization. The potential for misunderstanding is greater if a Subject is under stress, irritable, has low ego-strength, hyper-sensitive to perceived hurt, or is paranoid. If humor is employed, it is best to use ironic humor (dry, incongruous, surprising, cynical, and that comes at it by stating its opposite or by indirection). For example, "Things aren't what you'd call terrific so far today," "Not like winning the lottery, huh?" "Wanna hear something dumb? I thought today was gonna be an easy day." "Life keeps coming at ya'." "Too bad you never learned to duck." "As if things aren't bad enough. If we're lucky it'll get worse yet."

Self-Disclosure

There are mixed opinions about the use of self-disclosure in psychotherapy – a very unique relationship – that are not applicable here. Its use in crisis negotiations seems ideal in that it is a quick pathway to a serviceable rapport. Self-disclosure can build "bond and trust" (FBI) by finding common ground ("Me too"). It may encourage the Subject to respond in kind (models a desired behavior in others) while humanizing the Negotiator ("I'm a cop but I'm a husband and a father too – I'm a person just like you."). A NYPD Inspector said, "I like to tell my guys: Bring yourself into it. If he says, 'Oh, I'm having problems with my wife,' say, 'Yeah, I have problems with my wife too. My wife just yelled at me yesterday. . ." (Ruderman, 2012).

With self-disclosure, certain considerations should be taken into account to ensure the Negotiator's safety, security, and privacy (revealing what you choose, protecting what you choose). Disclosures should be about oneself, one's own feelings, thoughts, opinions, observations, actions. Names of family members, addresses, indiscretions, etc., or anything that might identify or compromise the Negotiator and/or his or her family should be out of bounds. Appropriate self-disclosures such as: "I too was depressed when I got back from Iraq." "After my divorce, I got serious about health and fitness. Now I work out three times a week." "It seems to me that politics has gotten uglier." "You said you were having a hard time with your kids. Parenting is the hardest job I've ever taken on."

Shading the truth or stretching it to make that connection should follow the same cautions discussed in the section on "Lying."

Avoid jargon and acronyms (cop talk) such as, "The CIT officer is on her way." CIT (Crisis Intervention Team) may not mean anything to a Subject and he or she may be reluctant to ask, perhaps because he or she thinks he or she should know but does not, or, alternatively, may be put off by it because of a lack of understanding (What's a crisis anyway?) or negative connotations ("I don't want to talk to no shrink"). Jargon, or police shorthand, creates barriers between parties (in-group/out-group) that may interfere with rapport-building. Similarly, avoid *legalisms* such as perp (perpetrator), plaintiff, etc., as they are rarely helpful, except when the Subject uses it first; even then, it puts the dialog on a different plane.

What Not to Say

- *Don't be stupid* or *This was a stupid thing to do.* "Stupid" is a loaded word that is both judgmental and insulting. To call a thing stupid will be heard by the Subject as calling him or her stupid. Name calling is never a good idea, but for a person who likely has low self-esteem, it may be devastating. They have a pretty good idea that what they are presently doing is stupid – that is, it has compounded their previous actions (e.g., drinking on the job and getting fired) and has made everything worse. Bad judgment is likely a trait of theirs and this would not be the first time they felt stupid and were called stupid by someone.
- *Have you done other dumb things like this before?* (as with stupid).
- *Let's get this over with* or *Can you speed it up a little. We've got kids getting out of school in ten minutes.* The Subject is at the center of the chaos he or she has created; school kids and waiting parents are not part of their present concern. Rushing the Subject will be perceived by him or her as disrespectful, a bad thing when trust-building is the objective. He or she will push back. Feeling out-of-control, as it is, the Subject will likely do what he or she is doing at his or her own pace and in his or her own way, at least partly as a way of gaining control. "Get it over with" too can easily be misunderstood; "get things to work out for everyone concerned" or "settle things peacefully" are more positive alternatives.

- *Relax.* Telling a person to relax is rarely helpful. First of all, wishing does not make it so, and second, it may increase the Subject's dis-ease as she or he tries hard to do so.
- *You've made a hell of a mess of this.* Blaming and put-downs that make a person feel worse about his or her predicament, even if true, while in the midst of it, tell him or her what he or she already knows can only serve to deepen shame; it damages a collaborative bond between Subject and Negotiator.
- *Is there anyone you'd like us to call when this is all over? resolved?* "All over" is another one of those loaded terms to be avoided. Projecting the end of the incident into the future is not a bad idea, but "suggesting" a positive or hopeful outcome would help, e.g., "When we are all safe and you feel okay with the way you helped make things turn out" would you like me to let somebody know you're okay?" "All over" might sound more like a bad ending than a resolution; resolution is too much like jargon or "psychobabble."
- *Don't worry. Everything's going to be all right.* Don't give false hope. Don't gloss over reality. The Subject will be sensitive to the falseness and insincerity. It is condescending and flip and thus undermines the crucial trust and respect necessary for rapport. The Subject is likely to feel discounted.
- *What have you done to those hostages in there?* Beware of accusatory language that is likely to arouse the Subject's defenses. "Do you, or does anyone in there, need medical assistance?" Questions usually are less threatening than statements. In "need of medical assistance" deliberately begs the issue of whether or not the Subject has harmed anyone. Besides, a hostage with an emergent or existing or medical condition may be in need of medical assistance through no direct fault of the Subject (if you don't count that he is holding someone against their will).
- *Why don't you send those people out?* It's all in the timing. Not bad in itself, but it is better to ensure that there is a sufficient enough rapport to make the request seem reasonable and not high-handed.

Signs of Rapport and Indicators of Progress

Signs that a rapport has been established may include: a change in the Subject's manner toward the Negotiator, i.e., warmer, friendlier, or at least less combative; a change in the way the Subject addresses the Negotiator, i.e., less formally, as by name instead of officer; the Subject initiates more and elaborates instead of responding to questions, i.e., volunteers information, gives more details; verbalizes feelings of attachment or dependency, i.e., "Will you be at the hospital when they take me there?"; verbalizes curiosity and interest in the Negotiator, i.e., "How old are you? You said you were in the Marines. Were you in the war?"

Rapport is not a finite or unchangeable state, it may be deep or shallow, enduring or transient; it requires reinforcement and maintenance throughout. How do you know whether or not progress towards a working rapport has been made? Some indicators of progress are (Source for some data: FBI/Critical Incident Response Group-Crisis Negotiation Unit):

Content of Subject's *Communication* – shift away from threatening or violent language (mellowing through developing relationship), spontaneous expressions of attachment to Negotiator, e.g., "You're OK, not like other cops I know"; "I won't talk to you. I'll only talk to John."

Form of Subject's *Communication* – shift to lower vocal volume, slower rate of speech, responses become more detailed, elaborated, and longer, Subject increasingly initiates conversation rather than waiting to be questioned (after a break in contact), increased willingness or desire to speak to Negotiator(s), i.e., "Where were you? What took you so long? I had a lot to tell you";

Behavioral – violent behavior stops or is reduced, hostages are released, and deadlines pass without incident (can be interpreted as an indicator or measure of Subject's degree of engagement with the Negotiator and perhaps as a "gift" to the Negotiator, *See, now we're even – you did something for me and now I did something for you*");

Increased Willingness to Follow Negotiator's *Suggestions* – verbalizes desire to see no harm come to hostages, talks projects to incident resolution, e.g., surrender process (can be interpreted as an expression of feelings of safety and trust in the Negotiator and his or her ability, through their agency, to bring a face-saving resolution).

SUMMARY

Building rapport is the first task of a Negotiator as rapport is the prime and essential ingredient in an intervention. A Subject is more likely to negotiate, even his or her own safety, with someone in whom they have a measure of trust, think sincere, and can relate to. It is the foundation on which all other stages are built.

How Negotiators' relate, their manner and the means can aid or, conversely, spoil the potential for resolution of the incident. Some of those factors for verbal crisis communication are highlighted. Generalizations about what to do and what to say, or not do or say, are just that – generalizations; as such, they provide good guidelines for Negotiators that fit many, even most, but not all. Flexible and creative Negotiators may find that "breaking the rules" for a given Subject in a given set of circumstances is best, sincerity, tolerance, the ability to suspend judgment, and respectful engagement are, perhaps, *the* key rapport-building behaviors and *Negotiator* qualities.

Rapport, once established, must be maintained throughout the incident. In the course of the negotiations, the rapport may become the basis for a Negotiator's influence and a Subject's compliance.

Throughout the course of the rapport building stage of our crisis intervention model important information that is part of the assessment may have been revealed. A fuller, more complete assessment is in order to plan strategy and tactics and to restore stability and ensure the safety of everyone concerned; false or incomplete information can lead to serious missteps.

Chapter 3

STAGE II: CONDUCT CRISIS, BIOPSYCHOSOCIAL AND LETHALITY ASSESSMENT

OBJECTIVE: "Plan and conduct crisis and biopsychosocial assessment including lethality measures" (Roberts & Ottens, 2005).

Misjudgments, failed strategies, and miscommunications may result from faulty conclusions based on an inadequate or incomplete assessment of the situation or the person. Premature judgments are often based on *confirmation bias* (where perceptions are skewed by a bias going in and where "proof" is sought for what has already been concluded) – it supports what you thought going in rather than what you learned once you got there. As such, errors are likely; in critical negotiations, life and death decisions that are off the mark may have very serious consequences. Realistically, complete assessments are not possible given the amount of time they take and the inexpertise of the Negotiator versus the clinician (mental health professional); the intrusiveness of a formal assessment may damage the rapport with its one-sided agenda and interrogatory format. In crisis situations, where quick action in an uncertain and volatile time frame may be called for, assessments by necessity must be incomplete – "quick and dirty." Negotiators need to seek and listen for critical information in a timely manner. However, when feasible, and rapport appears to be particularly important to the Subject, and is effectual, it is best to allow the Subject to tell his story allowing relevant data to emerge more naturally; a spare use of minimal encouragers and other active listening techniques will promote elaboration of data and details.

Roberts and Ottens model (2005) places *assessment* in the first of their seven stages followed by *rapport building*. Their order is problematic for me. For me, *rapport* is the first step, the foundation upon which trust is built, which frees-up the Subject to be receptive to a Negotiator and to begin to reveal himself. (And so, I have modified the order, placing rapport building first; the reader may have it either way). This may all be moot because as Roberts and Ottens (2005) proffer, *rapport building* and *assessment* are in reality "entwined":

> Rather than grilling the client (read: Subject) for assessment information, the sensitive clinician or counselor (read: Negotiator) uses an artful interviewing style that allows this information to emerge as the client's (read: Subject) story unfolds. A good assessment is likely to have occurred if the clinician has a solid understanding of the client's situation, and the Client, in this process, feels as though he has been heard and understood. Thus, it is quite understandable that in the Robert's model, stage I – Assessment and Stage II – Rapidly Establish Rapport are very much intertwined. (p. 334)

A full assessment is an unlikely and unrealistic under crisis conditions, and may not even be desirable; it may offer too much information for a Negotiator not trained as a MHP (mental health professional), and its conduct will alter the tone and distract from the objective of the negotiations, the primary and immediate goals of safety and short-term situational resolution.

Assessments can be direct or oblique and both may benefit from a preface – a word or two to lead-in eases the intrusiveness and seeks to excuse it, asks permission to do so (or gives the Subject permission to *not* answer). Asking for permission is respectful and disarming and gives the Subject some measure of control by choosing to not answer (something she or he already has, has always had) – you cannot make someone talk who is determined not to. It is a way of offering a good reason for asking questions while acknowledging the Subject's right to answer or not (autonomy and control) thus reducing his or her felt need to resist the Negotiator's authority and intrusiveness ("Is it okay if I ask you about. . ? I ask because it'll help me to . . . You don't have to but I'd really like to know"). Respectful but not fawning – it creates a "communication climate" or "social tone" (Adler, 2004) that is constructive, and is likely to be felt and reciprocated in kind.

Hostage situations, in order to be successfully negotiated, require a two-pronged assessment. One-prong probes for information about the Subject, the other about the situation or surround. Of course, they are in reality inseparable. It is just that in a crisis situation *the situation* assumes a greater importance, a more central importance, than it would in a clinically-oriented assessment.

Situational Incident Assessment

The *Situational Incident Assessment* below is a crisis assessment that deals with both the situation and the Subject at the center of the crisis.

Situational Incident Assessment[1] would include these elements:

Type of Incident – incidents can be classified as hostage or nonhostage types, barricade, barricade with victims, and with or without suicide threats or a presumption of such, e.g., suicide by cop. Kidnapping, a crime where the location of the Subject and victim is unknown by the authorities is necessarily treated similarly but separately. The Crisis Negotiation Team acts in an advisory capacity rather than a controlling one.

Crisis Site – the location, or site, of the incident (there may be more than one for a mobile Subject or if a criminal act occurred prior to the present standoff). The location of the crisis site, and other incident-related sites, impact on logistical, forensic, and tactical decision making.

Person(s) Held – Is the Subject holding others against their will? Are those persons known to the Subject? Relatives? Domestic partners? Associates? Is the hostage/victim a stranger? Was the hostage especially chosen for a purpose or was it an opportunistic or adventitious grab?

Degree of Violence – Has the Subject made threats of violence? Have the threats been global or specific? Has he or she carried out those threats? Has the violence resulted in injury or death or property destruction? Is the violence mild, moderate, serious or lethal? By what means (weapon?)?

Initiation of Incident – Who sounded the alarm? Was it the Subject herself, a hostage/victim, a neighbor or bystander? How were authorities made aware of it – 911, other?

---

[1] Source: FBI/CIRG/CNU.

Preparation – Planned or unplanned, intended or unintended? Is the current situation the result of an orchestrated plan; the unintended consequence of a criminal act, an impulsive or spontaneous act, misadventure, the acting out of a psychotic thought process (delusional or hallucinatory)? If planned, is it crudely or carefully planned – well thought out?

Demands – Has the Subject verbalized demands for the release of hostages or for the police to leave? Are there other demands – instrumental or expressive? – realistic? Substantive? Vague? Irrational or bizarre? Do they suggest or reveal a Subject's agenda?

Timing of Violence – Has there been threats or acts of violence? Was the violence enacted at the outset or after contact? Relative to a demand? Posturing? Believed to be meant to provoke a police response, e.g., suicide by cop, or to make a point?

Deadline – Has the Subject set deadlines? Are they specific? Precise? Consistent or changing? Have they been kept to or allowed to pass without incident?

Subject's Demeanor – what is the Subject's audible emotional tone or state? What is the predominant emotion depression, hostility, anxiety, agitation, flat or bland, detached? Is it appropriate (does it fit the situation)?

Degree of Communication – talkative (or manicky) versus thoughtful (or taciturn)? Does Subject volunteer or elaborate freely or does the Negotiator have to question and prompt constantly? What is the Subject's communication style; what if anything can be concluded from the Subject's degree of communication?

Suicide – Are there threats, hints, failed attempts or gestures, predictions, means? What is the likely immediate impact of a Subject's suicide on hostages or others, on the negotiation strategy? What is known about the Subject's history of depression, suicidal threats, attempts, and gestures, including means? Is suicide by cop likely?

Threats – Have threats of any kind, especially violent acts against the self or others, been made? Are threats realistic, likely, empty, bizarre, confused, incoherent, delusional? History of violence? How will these threats affect negotiation strategy?

Criminal History – What is known of a Subject's criminal history may answer any number of questions about his trajectory, penchant for violence, criminal sophistication and versatility, known associates. Does it suggest a picture of mental illness or psychopathy? Has the Subject been involved in a barricade or hostage situation previously? What was the outcome? Were there special circumstances? Incarceration: home or work release, penitentiary (minimum, medium, maximum) Adjustment?

Loss – Is the Subject known to have suffered loss recently or in the past that may be considered traumatic, e.g., loss of a child, parent, partner, in war? Are there lingering aftereffects, i.e., PTSD-like symptoms?

Drugs and/or Alcohol – Is the Subject exhibiting signs of current or recent alcohol or other drug ingestion? What kind of substance(s)? What are the effects of that substance on users, this Subject in particular? Is the Subject a user, abuser, addict? How will that affect this Subject, in this incident, either through his use or withdrawal? Does the Subject have access to his substances of abuse? When was he last dosed? Has he made demands for preferred substances of abuse? Has this been planned for? Is a medical or poison control consult lined up?

Escape – Does Subject have a history of escape attempts or successful escapes from custody or containment? By what means and degree of wiliness? Are the perimeters in place and secure?

Environmental Supports – Is the Subject employed? Is she in an intimate relationship? What is the state of that relationship? Positive family support? Social organizational membership? Ties to the community? Friends, coworkers?

Stressors – What stressors are currently impinging on the Subject? Are any of them the precipitants of this incident? How significant are the stressors for the Subject?

Medical – Does the Subject have medical issues and concerns? Illness – chronic, serious, debilitating, terminal? Does Subject's medical condition require attention now or soon? Need for medical consult? Prescriptive medication – type, effects, dosage, last dose taken, addiction?

Coping methods – What are Subject's usual means of coping? How effective generally? Presently? Means?

Resources – Like environmental supports, but of the personal and individual nature?

Strength of character – personality? Intelligence, resilience, flexibility? Positive accomplishments and life experiences to draw upon?

Some opening lines or prefaces that ease the burden of assessment for Subject might sound like these samples:

- "If I ask too many questions then just say so." (Just verbalizing his irritation and registering his complaint may be enough to push through it.)
- "Don't tell me more than you want or think I have a need to know." (Giving permission for the Subject to do what he didn't need your permission for in the first place – a feeling of having some control of the situation.)
- "I might ask you some things that make you uncomfortable. Tell me so, but don't let that keep you from telling me your side of it." (Acknowledges their discomfort but appeals to their need to air their story.)
- "I might ask you some things you don't want to talk about. Do or don't. It's up to you." (Again, permission.)
- "I'll only ask you about stuff in your best interest – that could help you out. You can be the judge." (Again, appeals to their desire to be heard and to advance their "cause.")
- "If I ask you about you it's only me trying to find us a good way out of this." (The use of "us" implies a partnership and promotes the rapport.)
- "My mother used to say, 'You learn more by listening than by talking.' She was right and I'm here to listen." (Folksy. Recalls mother-child bond while offering to listen – a good offer for someone who likely feels unheard – something begun in childhood.)
- "My mother used to say, 'You learn more by listening than by talking.' I guess it never took." (Tries to soften and mitigate the many questions with humor.)
- "My mother used to say, 'You learn more by listening than by talking.' "I can't figure how you can listen if you don't ask some questions." (Again, to soften the intrusion of questioning.)
- "My mother used to say, 'Don't ask so many questions. You learn more by listening than by talking.' Sorry if it feels like too many questions." (Again, to soften the intrusion of questioning.)
- "I learned a long time ago that everybody has a story to tell. Tell me about yourself." (Your offer to listen to his/her side of it may be a first for him.)

It is axiomatic that the more information you have about a Subject the better able you are to craft an effective intervention, up to the point where it becomes too much information (more than you need or not immediately relevant). Too much information can cloud the most immediately relevant information and clog the avenue to action. For practical reasons, we strive for an assessment that is as complete as it needs to be and is, at the very least, *sufficient* to meet our primary purpose: the preservation of life, the restoration of the Subject's precrisis stability and functioning, and, the partial and temporary, short-term resolution of a personal crisis that is being acted out on the public stage. Time strictures, the interrogatory nature of mining for information (with so many questions asked it can sound too much like a clinical interview, or worse, like a police interrogation), and the hypersensitivity of the Subject (paranoid, obsessive, and irritable Subjects may be least tolerant of questioning); it is an inherent problem in crisis assessment, and so, a briefer more cogent query is called for. An assessment conducted amidst an active crisis should necessarily focus on the most essential information needed to plan and intervene effectively. Other relevant information that may not be immediately needed to meet the essential goal, i.e., the preservation of life, is stored, as it may later prove useful as the situation unfolds or changes.

Assessment, an orderly gathering of information relevant to a Subject's current situation, which includes both historical and current information is used to formulate working hypotheses about the individual and their situation, and plan a negotiation strategy. It is an ongoing process that continues throughout the negotiations; as new information emerges or significant Subject behavior is made manifest, the CNT considers its meaning and import and integrates it with what is already known; the negotiator updates and amends his hypotheses about the Subject, the situation, and how to proceed.

Assessment of the Person

Realistically, assessing the situation and the person is largely entwined, making the two co-occurring. In a good assessment, information on both should emerge smoothly. In line with the crisis intervention principle of providing safety and preserving life first, lethality, medical and mental health concerns, and alcohol or drug ingestion/intoxication are most cogent and should be paid special attention. Lethality, or dangerousness to self or others, is the most pressing concern (and may be the underlying crisis itself; the risk for suicide or homicide may escalate for a Subject in crisis with attending medical needs, over time. Health issues should be accounted for carefully as the assessment shifts from the situation to the person.

Medical need might include injuries sustained in the course of the current incident, chronic conditions. Where medication or injury/illness management issues are present, including availability of prescriptive drugs (last dose, consequences of missed dose, food or fluid intake, etc.) and/or alcohol or drug intoxication affects a Subject's thinking, judgment, inhibition (control versus impulsivity), and the ability to act deliberately, e.g., coordination, a medical consult is called for. Assessment of medical conditions (presence and status), including prescriptive drugs, physical and psychological trauma treatment, and dietary concerns, i.e., diabetes, of hostages, too, must be done. This is a necessary humane consideration that is, at the same time, a potential negotiating tactic; a hostage-taker does not want the burden of an injured or sick hostage, whose condition will likely worsen over time. A Negotiator may well be able to bargain for the release of the "sick woman."

Mental health concerns affect a Subject's capacity for rational thought, and the presence of delusions and hallucinations may lead him/her to act in ways that constitute dangerousness. Psychotropic medication and maintenance issues also call for psychiatric and psychological expertise. While this assessment is of the Subject, the health concerns of the hostages is of parallel importance — preserving life refers to all of the parties to the incident including hostages, first responders, and bystanders.

In an assessment of the person, the focus is on the Subject rather than on the situation, although realistically, they cannot be separated; it includes the following elements, some of which overlap with a situational assessment, observation, collateral interviews and other sources of information gathered through record checks, etc. Additional information on the Subject may be found in local records searches, and in a protracted incident, remotely stored records, e.g., out-of-state college transcripts and disciplinary actions taken, military DD214s.

The following topic headings represent an orderly assessment protocol:

Identifying Data – includes name, AKA, DOB, addresses (present, previous), home, mobile, and work phone; physical description, tattoos, marital status, and next of kin, SSN.

Medical – includes current acute conditions (illnesses, disorders), chronic conditions, especially those requiring on-going monitoring and medication maintenance (diabetes: blood glucose testing and insulin); disabilities (limitations); history of medical hospitalizations and surgery.

Psychological/Psychiatric – includes history of inpatient (hospitalization) and outpatient treatment (community mental health activities), e.g., individual, group, marital/family therapy, substance abuse counseling, and self-help programs; attitude toward mental health treatment, current or past and how well-thought of, name former and current practitioner, diagnosis and medication history of violence, dangerousness to self or others, and characteristic coping methods may be helpful.

Criminal History – includes number of arrests, age at time of arrests, felony charges, dispositions: convictions-acquittals, sentences (jail, prison, probation, suspended); total time served, institutional adjustment.

Employment History – includes occupational title, type of work, licenses-certifications, job changes (longevity, frequency of change), promotions, work behavior (argumentative, fighting, reliability, trustworthiness, complaints of sexual harassment or racial, religious, gender bias and intolerance. Adjustment in the workplace is the source of important information about the Subject's attitudes, social skills, maturity, and personality. Position and type of work are estimate measures of education and intelligence.

Military Service – includes years of service (active and reserve), overseas deployments, combat, trauma (physical/mental), awards and decorations, military occupational specialty (MOS) – duties explained with special attention paid to military police – criminal investigative training, weapons/explosive-demolitions specialties, and special warfare training (sniper, special operations); some MOSs, because of the high level skills and/or education/training required may help a Negotiator estimate the Subject's intellectual capacity.

Years of service and rank at discharge can be a measure of the individual's adjustment, i.e., a soldier's rank below sergeant (E-5) after ten-years of service suggests disciplinary problems, alcohol/drug problems, authority problems, poor performance, or low intelligence, poor leadership skills. The nature of the discharge itself can tell an interviewer a lot about the Subject's service.

Social Relationships – current committed relationship (married, live-in, hetero- or homosexual orientation? Other gender category? Dependent children (ages, degree of involvement whether living in the home or not, payment of child support problems), family of origin (parents, siblings: numbers, ages, whereabouts, closeness-closest), friends (who, where). How much, if at all, are any of these relationships (includes friends, family, organizations, coworkers) social supports for the Subject? Can these resources and social relationships be mobilized to support the Subject through his current situation?

Abuse History – includes Subject's history of abuse as a child victim and adult perpetrator. Both are revelatory of current psychological adjustment and point Negotiators toward conflict areas and triggers ("hot buttons") that the Negotiator may choose to avoid, or, alternatively, exploit. Resentment, anger, guilt, and difficulty with authority figures are likely features of this Subject's emotional life.

Environmental Supports and Stressors – knowledge of the stressors in the lives of Subjects and supports available to them aid the Negotiator in assembling an equation – the events and relationships that impinge upon a person with stress-inducing effects, on one side and, on the other side, the people, organizations, and institutions that are available to him to counter-balance the effects of the stress. One may find solace in their religion after the death of a parent and comradeship with other veterans at the local VFW post.

The Triage Assessment Form: Crisis Intervention (Myer, Williams, Ottens, & Schmidt, 1993, Pazar, N. D.) – was developed to sort out the most urgent needs to be addressed as a hierarchical priority – suicidal danger takes priority over a broken leg. It measures three domains or critical areas of mental functioning: *cognitive* (thinking), *affective* (feeling), and *behavioral* (doing). Each is scored according to a severity scale, a measure that reflects the level of impairment. The procedure takes some training and practice, and may not be useful for most Negotiators except to aid them in focusing on a Subject's thinking, feeling, and relevant behavior. A rough estimate of the Subject's functional level (functional versus impairment) can be made simply by rating his or her control in each domain on a scale of 0–10 (0=low impairment, 10=severe impairment). For the purposes of the Negotiator and his/her task, such an estimate will be subjective, based on some internal measure. For example, a cognitive domain scale of impairment rated by a Negotiator as "6" might translate to "not good but still pretty much intact." Similarly, a rating of "8" might translate to "he's a mess. I'm going to have to speak slowly and break things down into bite-sized pieces." Much more useful operational language.

LETHALITY

Lethality, in the context of crisis negotiations, refers to the Subject's risk for dangerous behavior including: parasuicide (self-mutilation, suicidal gesturing, suicide, assault or homicide, or for provoking a tactical police response that could lead to injury or death of any of the parties, i.e., the Subject (suicide by cop), hostages, police and other emergency responders, and bystanders.

The current incident, be it a hostage, barricade, or suicide threat is the first evidence of a Subject's propensity for violence. What remains to be uncovered is how much more likely, in what way, and directed toward himself or someone else?

A lethality assessment can be a narrow, stand-alone inquiry or a subset of a fuller one, such as, a biopsychosocial assessment. Both address concerns about a Subject's state of mind specifically regarding thought and intent to do harm. It asks, "Are you thinking about killing yourself or someone else?"

There are very many factors that impact upon the risk of suicide for all Subjects, including: separation-divorce; depression; unemployment; serious, chronic, or terminal illness; delusions and/or hallucinations; feelings of guilt, hopelessness/helplessness, unworthiness, smoldering or overcontrolled anger; significant alcohol-drug abuse or addiction; PTSD; a recent significant loss (this is not an all-inclusive list). Information on these factors is derived from the *Situational* and *BioPsychoSocial* assessments presented above; again, assessments overlap and have multiple applications.

If a Subject's statements directly or indirectly express thought and/or intent to suicide or seriously harm another, evidence a number of the above factors, or express overconcern with death, or he or she refuses or avoids answering direct questions about the above, associated factors, a direct lethality probe is called for. A direct lethality probe involves confronting the Subject bluntly (not gruffly though) about their thoughts, feelings, and intentions with regard to suicide, assault, or homicide. It is too important to tip-toe around or gloss over. Resist the temptation to soften the probe's directness.

The objective of the probe is to get unambiguous answers about a Subject's dangerousness to himself or others. Follow-up questions may be necessary to clarify a point and to encourage elaboration. The probe seeks answers to the following questions (see Part II, Chapter 10 for a fuller treatment):

- *Have you had thoughts of suicide/homicide?* – Thoughts precede action; the number of these thoughts, their frequency, the intensity, and the feelings they generate in the individual (how they feel about it) are indicators of greater or lesser risk.
- *Do you now have such thoughts?* – The immediacy of current thoughts of suicide or homicide makes for a volatility – the intensity of the moment can lead to an impulsive act or prompt some to act despite their own ambivalence. People may have those thoughts but do not intend to act on them.
- *Do you intend to harm yourself or someone else?* – A person may have suicidal/homicidal thoughts but clearly not intend to act on them; ironically, just having those thoughts can calm a person's emotional state.
- *If so, do you have a plan? What is your plan? When? By what means?* – Planning is further along than just thinking about "it." A plan with a lot of detail may be seen as a step yet closer. The means may indicate how realistic or potentially lethal an act may be.
- *Do you have access to those means that you say you have chosen?* – The presence of means or ease of access to the stated means aids the negotiation team's steps to plan or effect countermeasures.
- *Are your actions today part of a suicide (homicide) plan?* – Again, knowledge of the Subject's immediate plans aids the negotiation team to strategize the negotiations and prioritize actions.
- *Have you ever attempted suicide (assault, homicide) before? More than once? What happened?* – A Subject's history of suicidality may be of predictive value in the present.
- *What makes you choose death, yours or someone else's, over life?* – Such a question may be an opening to engage the Subject on his or her suicidal/homicidal thoughts or intents.

If a threat is more immediate, assessment should shift to intervention and crisis negotiation (quasi-treatment) to ensure the Subject's safety before continuing to assess, e.g., contract for safety.

Resistance

A Subject is likely to offer some resistance to the intrusiveness of a Negotiator's questions. We all are cautious and careful not to let ourselves become too vulnerable; self-protection and self-preservation are instinctual ("Don't tell too much, too soon, to anyone who is not trustworthy – maybe not even then"). Resistance can be anticipated and addressed before it becomes entrenched, and breached if it does. A good preface goes a long way in explaining why, apologizing for, and giving permission to do or not to do when it comes to questions that others may find personal and may be reluctant to answer. They can be set aside for the time being. In any case, expect some truths, some lies, some minimizing and some exaggerating depending upon the payoff for the Subject; with antisocial and psychopathic Subjects, expect few truths and many lies, minimizations, and exaggerations. (See, Slatkin, 2009, pp. 74–80 for a fuller treatment of countering resistance).

Beyond the Content

Our words say a lot about us. An awareness and analysis of a Subject's frequent use of certain words and their use of function words, such as verbs and pronouns, may reveal secrets about what a Subject is feeling, their self-concept, their social intelligence, and whether they are past, present, or future oriented. Complex thinkers will weigh different options and see a problem from different angles and perspectives, differentiate between them, use more complex words and engage in more dynamic and causal rather than categorical thinking (Pennebaker, 2011). Such observations aid the Negotiator in forming a deeper, more complex, and comprehensive picture of the Subject – *more and better data* to develop negotiating strategies.

Frequent silences, pauses, and hesitations may indicate uncertainty, ambivalence (mixed and conflicted feelings), intellectualizing (a cognitive style that chooses thoughts over feelings) that is a defense against Subject's feelings, or dissembling (contriving, deceptive responses for a number of reasons).

And so, the manner, tone, appropriateness, beyond the specific answers to questions – the information itself – are valuable sources of information. They may reveal a psychotic process – delusions and hallucinations – deception, various unhelpful defenses (that is, unhelpful in the present), e.g., denial or avoidance.

SUMMARY

Assessment in crisis situations should ideally be complete and in depth – the more information the better, up to a point. Realistically, time constraints and the intrusiveness of a more formal "interview-like" process can be off-putting, besides; there is such a thing as too much information – more than we need or can use. *BioPsychoSocial* and *Situational* assessments may yield much overlapping information, and so, should be modified so as not to be annoyingly repetitious. A lethality assessment is a stand-alone or a subset of the other assessments. Where events, observed behavior, and/or verbalized threats of violence point to elevated risk for suicide, assault, or homicide, a lethality assessment is called for; in such an event, the focus of assessment and negotiations shifts to intervention, e.g., contract for safety.

Assessment information is collected from all sources, collated, corroborated, integrated, and analyzed. Summaries based on the now processed information is disseminated to the negotiation team members who will utilize it to strategize the negotiations.

Chapter 4

STAGE III: IDENTIFY THE MAJOR PROBLEMS OR CRISIS PRECIPITANTS

OBJECTIVE: "Identify dimensions of presenting problems including the 'last straw' or crisis precipitants" (Roberts & Ottens, 2005).

How long has the Subject been in the grip of his dilemma? Did it happen rapidly and suddenly, catching him off guard and throwing him into a crisis or had it been building up over a long time – from a slow simmer to a rolling boil? Who else has been caught up in his melodrama or has been otherwise adversely affected by it? Had they seen it coming – imagined this scenario or one like it as the tragic if predictable outcome? What happened most immediately prior to the current circumstances and situation that may be thought of as a "last straw" – the precipitant that prompted this crisis? What are the manifest problems, the visible ones? The underlying problems? How far? How long? How deep? How broad? How intractable? How many others are affected? How many distinct problems, even if related? In other words, what are the dimensions of the Subject's problems and what can be said to have precipitated his or her current crisis?

Knowing the Subject's major problems and its dimensions can aid the Negotiator in devising an effective negotiation strategy, including planning for additional resources, e.g., child protective services, VA hospital care, etc. Identifying a focal point rather than floundering is more efficient and effective; it may point the way to negotiation "hooks" and possible informants or third-party intermediaries (TPIs) to call upon or to avoid. Hooks might include religious beliefs, love of parent, spouse, child, need to proclaim innocence or proclaim a cause, pride in job, military service. Potential TPIs might include relative, coworker, minister, former cellmate, defense attorney, etc. The number, degree, and nature of the problems, too, may signal whether a consultation with, for example, a medical, psychological, legal, or other professional is called for.

To state the obvious: "If you want to know, ask." It is also the case that "it" may be revealed – volunteered – as the Negotiator and Subject engage each other. A good starting point for inquiry in this phase is the Subject's conception of what has gone wrong and why? What does she see the problem(s) to be? How does she define the problem – her words are revealing and, additionally, give the Negotiator access to her personal vocabulary, e.g., "zoned out"; a Subject's personal vocabulary allows a Negotiator to join with them more smoothly by speaking their language. The Subject's revelations tell much about their insight, education, thinking, and, most importantly, whether they own their problems (take responsibility for) or blame others, an important consideration for negotiations. Subjects may parry inquiries or open up the flood gates – for some, the opportunity to tell their story, to ventilate, is welcome, as others in their life may have been unwilling to listen because they do not care or have given up on them over time having listened to the "same thing over and over again." Active listening skills remain central to managing the negotiations at this stage as well, as in all stages throughout.

As in the previous chapter on assessment, question sparingly but forthrightly. It can be helpful to tell a Subject why you are asking the questions you ask, to apologize for the number of questions (but generally not the questions themselves), and, where direct questioning of the Subject on matters held by him or her to be deeply troubling, tentativeness may be called for ("I wonder if in some small way could this be about things going on at work"). Very intimate questions should generally be avoided unless the Subject's volunteering of such matters opens up the discussion; even then, remember this is quasi-therapy and should not stray into unknown depths that get a Negotiator and Subject in over their heads. As the rapport grows, the Subject can be expected to open up more, although some areas may have to be put on hold and be revisited later, if at all.

Where feelings and concerns are openly expressed, active listening is employed to promote elaboration of detail and the ventilation of affect and allows the Negotiator to encourage the Subject and reinforce their verbalizations where appropriate. Where feelings and concerns are not acknowledged, or only very reluctantly and sparingly so, the Subject might lack the self-awareness (have a disconnect between their thoughts and feelings); be taciturn (temperamentally quiet – a man of few words); be suppressing painful feelings (consciously holding them down) or repressing them (unconsciously holding them down); or the rapport and trust is insufficient. Subjects with paranoid traits, in particular (for a full discussion of negotiating with paranoid Subjects, see Slatkin, 2010, pp. 103–104) do not open up, trust, nor talk about feelings because they feel exposed and vulnerable; talking about strong feelings may be difficult for anyone, but are especially so for someone who is extremely wary, suspicious, untrusting, and expects the worst from everyone. For reluctant or closed Subjects, the Negotiator may prompt them by initially verbalizing their feelings for them ("I would feel angry if I was in your shoes. Are you angry?" and, "The world of work can be a bitch. It has been for me at times."). Human emotions and concerns are universal and so they may be guessed at with a high degree of success. Of course, the more you know about the Subject the less guesswork. Some prominent problem areas follow, although any area or areas may be problematic for a particular Subject; some feelings, as noted, are usually associated with each area, although any and all may be present with any and all areas of concern. Once again, the areas overlap with those assessed previously. The Subject's earlier responses to assessment questions may simply have to be plugged in rather than queried over again:

Family – problems with child's school performance or behavior, discord between nuclear family members and parents or in-laws, child custody. *Associated Feelings*: frustration, anger, shame, regret, resentment, sense of failure, feelings of helplessness and hopelessness with or without suicidal ideas, fear of going crazy;

Marital – Sustained conflict or a recent incident, e.g., discovery of an affair, separation/divorce. *Associated Feelings*: depression, guilt, anger, remorse, frustration, gender hostility, jealousy, hostility toward partner, courts, in-laws, IRS, fear of going crazy, feelings of helplessness and hopelessness with or without suicidal ideas;

Relationship – Pattern of or recent or chronic conflictual, abusive or broken relationships. *Associated Feelings*: depression, guilt, anger, remorse, frustration, gender hostility, feelings of helplessness and hopelessness with or without suicidal ideas, fear of going crazy;

School/Work – School failure or loss of job(s). A recent failure or loss or a pattern of such. *Associated Feelings*: frustration, guilt, anger, resentment, embarrassment, damaged self-esteem (feels stupid), feelings of helplessness and hopelessness with or without suicidal ideas;

Financial – Credit card debt, home foreclosure, unemployment or underemployment. *Associated Feelings*: frustration, sense of failure, ego damage, sense of being overwhelmed, anxiety about future, feelings of helplessness and hopelessness with or without suicidal ideas;

Medical – From acute to chronic conditions that might range from bothersome to life-threatening. *Associated Feelings*: fear, anxiety, anger, adjustment difficulties, religious conflict within the self over articles of faith, fear of dying or disability and dependency, feelings of helplessness and hopelessness with or without suicidal ideas;

Legal – Civil or criminal court cases, incarceration which may or may not be a consequence of one of the other problem areas. *Associated Feelings*: fear of consequences (incarceration, prison assault), anxiety, anger, sense of being wronged, feelings of helplessness and hopelessness with or without suicidal ideas;

Alcohol or Drug Abuse – Use, abuse or addiction to alcohol or other substances that has caused problems in some or all of the other areas. *Associated Feelings*: frustration, shame, guilt, despair, self-hatred, feelings of helplessness and hopelessness with or without suicidal ideas, fear of going crazy;

Sexual – Might include any of the following: confused identity, closeted or coming-out homosexuality, sexual dysfunction or deviant urges/practices, inexperience-promiscuity, trauma (molestation in childhood, rape survival). *Associated Feelings*: panic, shame, embarrassment, guilt, spiritual distress, anger, low self-esteem, sense of self as damaged/worthless, fear of going crazy, feelings of helplessness and hopelessness with or without suicidal ideas;

Traumatic – If any or several signs point to trauma, PTSD should be considered (see Slatkin, 2009, pp. 106–110 for a full description of PTSD) along with or traumatic possibilities consistent with the assessment history. *Associated Feelings*: survivor's guilt, hostility (racial and/or gender), antiauthority, anxiety and depression, paranoia, constricted or numbed feelings, panic, fear of going crazy, feelings of helplessness and hopelessness with or without suicidal ideas.

Sample Dialog

Some suggestions for how to say or ask questions in this phase. Remember, some of these questions have already been answered conversationally and/or in other assessments:

- How do you make sense of it – this whole thing I mean?
- Before the earthquake, faint rumbles can often be heard.
- In your eyes, where and how did this begin?
- If you made a list of your problems – something we all could do – what would be at the top? Is that what this is about?
- Did you ever hear that old expression: "the straw that broke the camel's back" – what was your last straw?
- Who's to blame for today?
- Our complicated lives are made up of a lot of areas where problems could develop. Got an idea where your issues are?
- A big river is usually fed by lots of smaller rivers and creeks. If your river had a name what would it be? What about the smaller branches – what would they be called?
- If I asked your _____ (friends, spouse, parents, etc.) what would they say you were about?
- Did you have too much on your plate? What was on your plate? What took up a lot of what was on it?
- Who else beside you is going to feel the consequences of the leading up and the events of today? Have you thought about them and what it might mean to their lives?
- I'm confused. Why today and not yesterday or tomorrow?
- Do you (did you?) think that doing this would help or hurt your situation?

Every Negotiator must find their own voice – their way of speaking, manner, inflection. They need to be careful about using overused language, stilted speech, technical language or jargon; maybe worst of all, sounding scripted can easily be detected and can come across as insincere. Practice with the sample questions will lead to modifications that turn it into something uniquely yours – the same meaning but in a voice or manner that is yours – deliberate, empathetic, and sincere (Put yourself in the Subject's circumstances and mindset).

Collateral interviews seek new information and corroboration or contradiction of the Subject's claims. The Negotiator may ask the same questions asked of the Subject by substituting nouns or pronouns, i.e., "you" for "her." For example, "Did *she* have too much on her plate?"

SUMMARY

Assessment of the situation and Subject continues in this stage but becomes more focused on identifying the Subject's particular problem areas and how they are implicated, if at all, as a precipitant – the straw that broke the camel's back; what, why, in what way, how come, why now? Knowing the answers to these questions affords the Negotiator potential actions to take (strategies), possible hooks (avenues to explore), potential TPIs, and a lead-in to the "meat" of the quasi-therapeutic part of the negotiations (problem solving). Many of the questions have already been answered in the course of the previous stages – through dialog, assessment (biopsychosocial, situational, lethality), collateral and corroborative interviews, and a review of the Subject's records.

Chapter 5

STAGE IV: EXPLORE FEELINGS AND EMOTIONS

> Anyone can become angry – that is easy. But to be angry with the right person, to the right degree, at the right time, for the right purpose, and in the right way – this is not easy.
>
> Nicomachean Ethics, Aristotle

OBJECTIVE: "Explore feelings and emotions...." (Roberts & Otten, 2005).

Of the three realms of mental functioning: thinking, feeling, and doing, feelings – the emotional realm – is the most volatile. It not only includes the immediate feelings but underlying feelings – subconscious feelings – from past circumstances where similar or same such feelings were present: the anger over a particularly frustrating encounter with the court system ten years before is reawakened by a present crisis involving child custody and the courts – similar enough that the Subject's present feelings are colored by the first episode and the frustration and anger felt then is felt again. The present situation is as much fueled by the past as by the present. The Subject's unconscious feelings, those about which he may have no awareness, may nonetheless be driving or steering his or her present emotions and actions. The Subject's emotions are influenced by both past and present events and can, under critical circumstances, become too intense and may overwhelm his abilities to reasonably manage these, which may prompt him to act precipitously or with poor judgment. Some reasons to explore a Subject's feelings are:

- To encourage ventilation of feelings (ventilation can lead to an easing of the pent-up feelings and lessening the tensions);
- To encourage a Subject's awareness of his or her feelings (it is not unusual for people to be cut off or unaware of what he or she feels);
- To help a Subject understand his or her feelings understanding one's feelings and how they are tied in with his or her thinking, perceptions, expectations, etc. can lead to a clarity and more rational thinking – insight;
- To help a Subject regain control of his or her feelings (as with ventilation, control can be regained through the discharge and easing of pent up pressure);
- To encourage *more* or *less* expression of feelings (in a passive, depressed, or taciturn Subject greater expression may be encouraged by speeding up speech to re-energize the Subject or, alternatively, in an overly-emotional or overly-talkative Subject slowing speech down to discourage the expression of feelings may be desirable).

A word of caution! For many in our culture, men mostly, but it could be for anyone, who has learned at home, in childhood – by parental attitudes and teachings and, in the social milieu and culture at large – that feelings are feminine, scary, and best avoided; how feelings are dealt with is a big part of gender role expectation, for example, machismo. For all Subjects, a cautious test of their tolerance for their own feelings may be made:

1. *Listen to their verbalizations* – Do they use feeling words and label feelings?
2. *Observe their overt behavior* – Do they demonstrate affective behavior, e.g., laugh, cry, gesticulate, etc.? Do labelled feelings match the affect (says he is sad but laughs).
3. *Use feeling words and gauge its effect on the Subject.* How do they react, and do they respond in kind?

A good strategy for most Subjects, at least until a measure of their feelings of tolerance and comfort is established, is to begin with *thoughts* before broaching *feelings.* For example, "What did you *think* when your wife asked for a divorce?" versus "How did you *feel* when she asked you for a divorce?" You can plunge right in and see what happens (risky), gently probe through active listening for hints of feelings (better) and let the Subject initiate talk of feelings (best); the least coercive way is usually preferred. Of course, the Subject's temperament and current state will set the tone and point the direction and best approach for him or her.

Tentative and flexible approaches to broaching thoughts and feelings – some sample lines:

- I wonder if you thought about . . .?
- Could it be that your thoughts . . .?
- It might could be that (a Kentuckyism?) . . .?
- What if in some small way you . . .?
- Have you ever _____ (felt, thought) like this, maybe in a small way, a long time ago?
- What do you _____ (imagine, think, feel) others in your same situation might _____ (think or feel)?
- Our _____ (thoughts, feelings) can become confused when we're under stress. Are you clear, in your own mind what you really _____ (think, feel)?
- If you really felt _____ (angry, depressed, etc.) would you be able – willing – to say it out loud to someone, to me?
- Are you the kind of person who isn't quick to talk about your private thoughts or feelings?
- Is there someone in your life you can tell what you're thinking or feeling more easily? Who is that? What makes it easier to talk to _____ (her, him)?
- Have you told _____ how you feel? What do you think they would say?

Some Considerations

Generally, it is not a good idea to tell a Subject what to feel, e.g., "You should be. . . ." There are exceptions, as in the case of a Subject who appears to be unable to label his or her feelings for any number of reasons, e.g., a Negotiator might say: "If I were in your situation, I would be very. . . ." "In your situation, as you described it, I would feel _____. Is that what you're feeling?" "What do you think most people would feel in your situation? Is that what's going on with you too?"

However, telling a Subject what to feel can help a taciturn Subject own and label his or her feelings – a means of helping him or her to open up and better understand him/herself and the situation; it, too, is a way of normalizing the feeling (you are not crazy to feel this way) and, in effect, give the Subject permission to feel a certain way – "it's okay to feel disappointed."

The use of "should," too, is best avoided as it professes a right way to feel – an anathema to some Subjects. This is not a contradiction of the above. It simply restates the principle of choosing a deliberate response to a Subject based on which response better fits a given Subject in a given situation; some respond better to one over the other.

Dealing with emotions can be as difficult for some Negotiators as it is for some Subjects. Negotiators must be comfortable with themselves and their emotional lives and with the intense emotions of others; it is a bad practice for a Negotiator who is going through emotional upheaval in his or her own life to be employed in that role at that time. Being comfortable with his or her own feelings is a subliminal communication to the Subject that his or her feelings will be respected and that they are safe with the Negotiator. Also, it affords the Negotiator a safety barrier against being overinvolved and overwhelmed by the Subject's emotions and losing the perspective necessary to be effective. If a particular concern is raised by the Subject, for example, about her recent divorce, and the Negotiator is also facing divorce and/or has many leftover feelings concerning their own divorce, it might be advisable to change Negotiators (tell the team commander and sit it out!); however, on the other hand, in these same circumstances it might be the right match for that same reason. The guiding principle should always be a thoughtful, *deliberate*, and flexible response. Negotiators who become overinvolved and overidentify with the Subject can lose focus; conversely, a Negotiator who feels no empathy for the Subject may become overjudgmental and disapproving; neither are good matches for the Subject nor do they augur well for a good outcome. The *Secondary* Negotiator, Team Leader, and/or mental health professional should always monitor negotiations and Negotiator appropriateness and effectiveness.

Active Listening

Active Listening is the primary modality through which the exploration of feelings is accomplished. The Negotiator's use of *listening* techniques in particular encourages the elaboration of feelings (for a full discussion, see Slatkin, 1995, 2010). The Negotiator prompts the Subject to say more; hear their own words; make connections; be clearer; get in touch with their feelings; own their feelings; understand themselves more deeply; ventilate more fully; and, by giving voice to their feelings, get the reinforcement, acknowledgment, and validation they seek. Such goals lead to even greater ones – gaining control of and managing their emotions and the behaviors they lead to. Some select active listening techniques follow (Slatkin, 1995, 2010):

Reflection – Negotiator (active listener) "reflects" (mirrors) back to speaker his or her feeling as expressed by word or nonverbal cue:

>The Subject's feeling word is repeated:
>*Subject:* I'm mad as hell.
>*Negotiator:* You're mad as hell.
>A synonym is proffered:
>*Subject:* I'm mad as hell.
>*Negotiator:* You're very, very angry.
>From the Subject's tone, demeanor, facial, postural or other nonverbal cue, a feeling is conveyed that the Negotiator verbalizes:
>*Subject:* grits teeth, sneers, and clenches fists.
>*Negotiator:* Your look says you're very angry.

Clarification – Negotiator (active listener) hears Subject's expression of feeling, but, because it is ambiguous, unclear, or the Negotiator wants to highlight the feeling, he or she seeks to understand the Subject's meaning through clarification and elaboration.

>*Subject:* Life is over for me.
>*Negotiator:* By "over" do you mean you're thinking of ending your life? By "over" do you mean that it has changed such that there is no going back to the way things were?

Minimal Reinforcement/Encouragement – Negotiator responds to a Subject's expression of feelings by repeating the last word or using a "minimal" verbalization, such as, "Hum. Ah. Yeah" (nod, head shake). Its purpose is to encourage more elaboration or detail.

>*Subject:* I'm depressed.
>*Negotiator:* Depressed. Hum.

Summarization – Negotiator strings together a Subject's multiple, expressed feelings (more than one) and, by so doing, reviews, highlights and encourages his or her self-awareness.

> *Subject:* I'm unhappy. I'm no good at anything. Everything I do turns out rotten.
> *Negotiator:* You're sad and feel like a failure – like nothing you do works out the way you want it to.

Open-ended Probe – Negotiator asks a question of the Subject about his/her feelings to seek more information and to encourage more verbalization and elaboration ("Tell me more"). Also, as earlier stated, it's a rapport-builder, it conveys continued interest ("I'm still with you").

> *Subject:* I'm so mad I could do something I might later regret.
> *Negotiator:* I can't miss hearing how angry you are, but tell me how you got to be as angry as you are?

Closed Probe – A Negotiator seeks specific information or uses this limited query to help the Subject focus or to check out an understanding or to slow down a too talkative Subject.

> *Subject:* I can't get past my feelings for her.
> *Negotiator:* Your feelings? Do you mean love?

Confrontation – The Negotiator confronts, or challenges something a Subject has said (not the Subject, but what the Subject has said). It is one way a Negotiator helps a Subject to examine his or her verbalized feelings or behaviors, especially when they are contradictory. Its purpose is to prompt a Subject to explore and examine his or her feelings more closely.

> *Subject:* It takes a lot to make me angry.
> *Negotiator:* I'm struggling to understand you. You say it takes a lot to make you mad, but you've told me about six or seven instances when you lost your cool. A few minutes ago you blew up at me. Which is it?

Self-disclosure – A Negotiator, by revealing something about his/her feelings, models, encourages, and "gives permission" for a Subject to express his or her feelings. Its purpose is to help a reluctant, frightened, or defensive Subject express his or her feelings and concerns.

> *Subject:* It's hard to talk about.
> *Negotiator:* When my mother died I felt lost. It was almost a year before I could talk about it. It helped when I finally did.

Information Giving – Is to provide relevant new information or correct a Subject's misinformation:

> *Subject:* My parole officer has to lock me up for this.
> *Negotiator:* I spoke to her and she has the discretion to write you up without sending you back to prison if.... There is a new substance abuse program on Church St. with a very good success rate.

Reinforcement – Negotiator recognizes and encourages certain of a Subject's verbalizations or behaviors in the "right direction" – that is, those that are likely to move the negotiations toward a certain desired end. Reinforcement aims to encourage other similar words or acts.

> *Subject:* I guess I could let you send in some medicine for that sick boy.
> *Negotiator:* I know his mother will be grateful to you. That's a good thing you're doing.

Immediacy – The Negotiator verbalizes his or her feelings about something the Subject has said or done or left unsaid to bring out into the open unspoken feelings and to provide immediate feedback to the Subject about how he comes across and how his words or actions affect others.

> *Subject:* (seethes silently).
> *Negotiator:* You haven't said anything for five minutes, but I can feel your rage right through the phone. It makes me really uneasy.

Interpretation *(use with caution)* – The purpose here is to connect the dots for a Subject who may not be aware of or understand his feelings or actions. The Negotiator cautiously offers a possible explanation to a Subject for what their feelings mean.

> *Negotiator:* Perhaps your anger, which is very, very intense, has something to do with what happened to you in the army. That thing that happened to you then and what happened to you today at work are a lot alike.

Should you choose to question a Subject about his or her feelings, "Why" is rarely helpful in exploring feelings as people rarely know "why" they feel as they do. When pressed, they are likely to offer a reason why – usually "because" – usually a rationalization – that is, an excuse that has been conjured up after the fact to explain or justify the "why"; the real reason is often outside of their awareness – unconscious or subconscious. The immediate situation or event can be thought of as a trigger that prompts the feeling that is tied to what is underneath and not the "why" itself. All of this is not meant to exclude a simpler, more straight-line connection between a feeling and a "why" that can occur, it's just that humans are often more complex and multi-layered than that.

A more productive line of questioning that is likely to lead to exploration and elaboration might be: "In what way does _____?" "Where does all that self-pity come from?"

Reframing

Reframing is an effective way of off-balancing a person's held beliefs; as such, it challenges them to see a problem or solution in a different light – hopefully a healthier, more productive way and thereby *feel* differently – our thinking drives our feelings. For example, a Subject says, "She's always tearing me down." The Negotiator says, "She must really care for you to want you to be a better man – for you and for your marriage." Reframing can unstick a stuck Subject. Changing thoughts changes feelings and behavior.

Resistance

Resistant, blocked, stymied, deadlocked, at an impasse, etc., describes a state in which a Subject's unwillingness or inability to deal with his or her feelings pinches off the dialogue between Negotiator and Subject; it threatens to bring the negotiations to a halt and to fail altogether. The reason for such resistance may be conscious or unconscious: in a prison setting or with criminal Subjects, revealing certain information (or associated feelings) may be seen by them as detrimental to their charges or be perceived by others as a weakness; for other Subjects, the unconscious avoidance of painful feelings may cause them to shut down. There are several approaches and techniques for dealing with resistance, too large a topic to deal with here; for a full explanation of strategies, stratagems, and techniques, see Slatkin (2010).

SUMMARY

Exploring feelings with a Subject can be very challenging for both the Subject and the Negotiator. Feelings may be very foreign to a Subject – not that they are not present in everybody. Some people are less aware of their feelings, judge some of their feelings as okay or not-okay, have learned not to reveal them or may be temperamentally not given to talk much; angry feelings in particular have been singled out as "bad" and/or are scary because they may get out of control and lead to violent behavior or a sense of being "crazy."

Active listening remains the best means of helping a Subject acknowledge (and being heard) his or her feelings – a precondition of going further – and exploring, ventilating, utilizing, managing, and controlling them. Some specific techniques, including reframing are proffered. Starting with thoughts – "What do you think about that?" – before moving to feelings – "How does that make you feel?" – allows a Subject to ease into the more threatening zone of emotions.

Chapter 6

STAGE V: GENERATE AND EXPLORE ALTERNATIVES

OBJECTIVE: "Generate and explore alternatives (untapped resources and coping skills)" (Roberts & Ottens, 2005).

Under pressure – stress and strain – we can fold and break down, physically and psychologically, and end up in the vortex of a crisis, largely of out own making. As we try to make sense of it while embroiled in intense, overwhelming emotions and confused we ask, "What's going on? Where am I? How did I get here? What am I going to do? I tried everything. Nothing helped. There was nothing I could do."

While they tried far from everything they most likely repeatedly reused those longstanding, familiar, and characteristic coping methods, some of which may have once worked but no longer do, and others, despite the fact that they never worked. This represents a Subject's *characteristic* means of coping. In the absence of new ways, the courage to find new ways, and the motivation to risk new ways, the old ways become the default mode. New ways offer new opportunities to restabilize, regenerate, and return to precrisis levels of adjustment and function, and to exceed them. How we perceive our problems and address, while subjective, they can be more or less productive; positive attitudes and expectations are generally more helpful to someone trying to "get a grip." For example, the perspective of a confident and hopeful person differs vastly from that of a depressed, defeated one who thinks or feels that he has tried everything – exhausted his resources and sees no way out. One can approach problems more confidently and rationally and find the resources from within the self to cope more effectively; however, we are not all endowed with vast resources, confidence, and, in the throes of a crisis, are not at peak performance. A *Crisis Negotiator* can facilitate a Subject's discovery of ways and means, from within, other than what he or she is currently, and characteristically, doing. Whatever external events are at play in the crisis, the Subject has made it worse by dint of his bad judgment and worse acts – he has turned a misdemeanor into a felony. While he cannot control those events outside of himself, he can keep from making them worse, keep from becoming unbalanced and less well able to cope – that is, he can control himself if not the world around him; ironically, by his coping efforts, he can influence the world (not control it) – and those events outside of him – by what he says and does (and that comes from a rational, open, fearless, and creative use of the self).

Alternative or other means differ from the present, failed ones, which are at the crux of the problem. To state the obvious, regardless of the means the Subject has employed, they have not worked and continue to not do so. Other means may be more effective and a Negotiator may be able to facilitate the Subject's exploration and discovery of alternate and other means. The crisis begins when the Subject believes that he or she has no means, no other means, or no other means left. It is then in an attempt to cope with and win out over his problems that a Subject resorts to his or her characteristic means, the usual and familiar, even if they have failed to help in the past. It has been said that if you don't know where to go you can always "go crazy;" employing means that have always failed and usually make things worse even though they always fail and usually make things worse is "crazy." But what can you do when you don't know what to do?

Baseline

It is helpful to try to determine a Subject's usual, or characteristic, way of seeing problems and of coping – his baseline. How does she deal with crises? With depression? Loss? Conflict? Is this a person who becomes frustrated easily, gives up quickly, loses hope, blames others or resorts to childish fits, violence, despair? Does he examine his feelings and thoughts and think through possible courses of action? Is she an intellectualizer who denies her feelings and tries to be rational above all else while suppressing and denying her feelings. Subjects react and respond to feelings of being out of control in their way, one of many response patterns open to them – overwhelmingly, they choose their default, characteristic styles. Knowing a Subject's style and response set can help the Negotiator strategize an approach to problem solving with that particular Subject. The Subject says, "I *feel* out of control" the Negotiator asks, "Have you ever been in a crisis situation before? What do you usually do when you *feel* yourself losing control, falling down? On the slippery slope?" The Subject says: "I *think* I'm out of control, the Negotiator says: "What makes you *think* that?" In the preceding examples the Negotiator begins by using the Subject's operating mode (*think* or *feel*).

The Negotiator can enter into a collaborative exploration with the Subject to generate other means that may be more productive for him; if new means are found, the incident may progress toward resolution; even if new means are not found, the process itself can set the negotiations on a more rational problem-solving path, stimulate ideas, remotivate and reenergize the Subject, and increase hope – such changes in outlook may in themselves move the incident toward resolution.

By definition, a Subject in crisis "lacks the equanimity" [def. balance or calm emotions when dealing with stress (Roberts & Otten, 2005)] to see the larger picture or appreciate long-term consequences of his or her actions. Ironically, under the strain of crisis, when new ways may be most needed and despite a singular lack of success with the old ways and means of the past, she or he is most likely to hold on tightly to characteristic ways of coping and familiar means. In crisis negotiations short-term interventions that raise hope, offer a way out, or lower the level of tension or anxiety are problem-solving solutions (not always so for therapy).

The *problem-solving* stage developed out of the hard work of the earlier ones: joining with the Subject, working through his or her inflamed feelings, and gathering the history ("his-story") necessary to formulate a way to help this Subject get it right. It is a rational exercise in looking at how to do it – the ways and the means of it – the how to exit the situation, save face, preserve life, and end on a note that, while perhaps less than ideal, is one to which all parties can agree on in the moment.

Given the chaos of the crisis state, the Subject, despite his or her bravado and posturing or outward appearance to the contrary, does not know what to do nor how to extricate him/herself from the mess he or she created and is presently mired in. An orderly review of options will help the Subject stay on the path of rational problem-solving where an answer to "what to do" is more likely to be found. The Negotiator can lay out the possible steps and courses of action as an array – a dealt hand of cards – and help the Subject choose from among them; or generate ideas of their own from which to choose. An array might include, for example: a no-suicide contract, hospitalization versus incarceration, child safety, substance abuse treatment, social services, legal aid, financial counseling and/or assistance, arranging for his lawyer to oversee his safe exit, arranging for a relative to care for dependent children, allowing an injured hostage out, paying child support arrears, apologizing and making amends, etc.

Alternative Behavior and Options

Knowing a Subject's coping skills, which includes traits and characteristics in the three realms of mental functioning – *cognitive, emotional,* and *behavioral* – how and what they *think,* what they *feel* and how they manage those feelings, and what they *do* relative to what they think and feel. Some such qualities include clear thinking, problem analysis, sound judgment, ability to identify options, grasp of short- and long-term costs and benefits, flexibility, patience, frustration tolerance, intelligence, emotional control, tracking, task orientation, persistence, hardiness, ability to ask for help, openness, creativity, strong motivation, etc. Knowing a Subject's strengths and weaknesses gives the Negotiator clues to the Subject's capacity for change, and which strengths to rely upon and weaknesses to work around.

A very fruitful avenue of inquiry is determining what a Subject usually does in tough times, what he or she has done in the past that has or has not worked, and what he or she has done leading up to the present incident. The Negotiator should avoid suggesting things to a Subject that has already been tried or rejected, that is, unless you have a different spin on it, "I know you said you tried to apologize to her, but she wouldn't listen. What if you met with her and her pastor and apologized in his presence?" New ways not only open up possibilities but challenge a Subject's statement, "I've tried everything. Nothing works."

Brainstorming

Brainstorming is a technique commonly used in business, education, industry, sciences, the military, public policy forums, and law enforcement, etc., to generate ideas. At first, all inputs are invited without a filter – there is no discussion as ideas are thrown out and recorded. A second pass is then made whereby the list is pared down – duplications are eliminated and similar ideas are combined to create a manageable size list of the better ideas; those left standing are subjected to discussion and analysis, such as cost-benefit. For a Subject, this interactive process requires his/her input and ownership and assent. It is also an excellent format for a Negotiator's facilitation. Again, the meta-message is that there are options and avenues other than the destructive and unproductive one chosen by the Subject that precipitated the crisis. As above, it addresses the plaintive, "There was no other way. I had no choice. What else could I do?"

The Negotiator should "acknowledge" a Subject's verbalized, self-generated options as "legitimate," to the extent that they are the efforts of the Subject, *but* challenge them on their merit. And so, a Subject is reinforced for generating ideas and is treated respectfully – even for absurd or repulsive ideas – but his idea, not him, is questioned in a non-judgmental, no-nonsense way:

> *Subject:* I could just kill all the women.
> *Negotiator:* You could (he could!), **but** it would only make your situation worse. It won't help you get what you said you wanted to happen today.

Sample Interventions

"Let's brainstorm this. You know. Just throw out as many ideas as we can without saying "yes" or "no" at this point. Even "crazy stuff." Then we can sort through them, keep the best ones and throw out the others. After you have a few good ones you can weigh them and see what you come up with."

- What has worked for you in the past when you've been in a tight spot, backed against he wall, and trying to find a way out?
- What would you think about _____?
- Have you thought about _____?

- What's the up-side? What's the down-side?
- How will that affect _____?
- Can you think of a time when you were down and were able to find the strength to bounce back? Do you remember how?
- Now my situation was not just like yours but it helped me to _____.
- How will that make things better or get you what you said you want?
- What if you did what you said first but instead of _____ you did _____?
- Tell me about something you absolutely will not do.
- Can we look at some other ways out of this? You know, just brainstorm.
- May I make a suggestion?
- I've had some bad times, too. Can I tell you what I did to fight my way out of them? It worked for me. Maybe it will work for you.
- Don't be so sure there's no other way until you've looked for other ways. Sometimes it helps to have someone go through it with you.
- So far you've thought about: _____, _____, and _____. Which way seems best for you and your son?
- How can I help? I want to help. Would it be helpful if I. . . ?

Looking Backward, Looking Forward

The Negotiator's answers to, "I've tried everything. Nothing works. I don't know what to do. There is nothing left for me to do. I've lost all hope," may be found in a search of the past and/or a look toward the future. The past may hold a history of successes and happier times associated with persons or activities. Things from the past can rekindle more positive feelings and remind one of forgotten successes, large or small. A minds-eye journey to the future reawakens lost hopes and dreams – things left to be pondered or accomplished – reacquaints one with once hopeful, happy feelings; dreams can soothe, open up, and spark possibilities, and may encourage future-oriented action ("When this is over . . .").

In either case, an exploration can open-up the dialogue and provide a set of images that can be subtly "guided" ("Can you picture yourself holding your little boy?") or "reframed"("You're calling it a failure, but just getting back on the field after twisting your ankle sounds like true grit to me").

Sample Dialogs

Looking Backward Dialog:

- What did you use to do as a kid that felt good – was fun?
- What was your favorite after school activity? What did you do on Saturdays?
- Everyone's good at something. What were you good at? What are you good at?
- What's your best success? Ever win any awards?
- Remember what it felt like to be happy? To be good at something?
- What would it take to make you feel good like that again?
- When was the last time you shot hoops?
- This is not your first rodeo. What did you used to do when you were in a bind and stuck for what to do?
- What worked for you in the past? What would happen if you took it up again?

Looking Forward Dialog:

- We never get it all done. What remains for you to get done?
- Are there loose ends to be tied up?
- You had dreams about the future, we all did? Do you remember yours? Can you still chase some of it?
- What could you still reasonably do after we finish here today?
- When you think about what you accomplished, and what you'd still like to accomplish, what comes to mind?
- Are there wrongs to be righted, apologies and amends to be made, family or friends to reconnect with?
- What would the best case scenario after today look like?
- Were there people in your life who inspired you? Ever thought of tracking them down?

Giving Advice

A Subject's coping skills, adaptability, and ego-strength can be estimated from his self-report, as well as from other respondents, by, for example, knowing what measures he or she may have already taken and whether they succeeded or not. History, too, is a good, if fallible, predictor of future behavior. It is a potential misstep on the part of the Negotiator to suggest an action to a Subject who has previously tried that very thing unsuccessfully. As stated before, knowing what a Subject has tried allows the Negotiator to avoid the pitfall of giving bad advice or offering tired options that may only irritate or frustrate a Subject who has become hopeful that the Negotiator might be of help: "I tried that. It doesn't work. Is that the best you can do? You're no help at all." Where advice or alternatives and options are called for, a Negotiator's knowledge of the Subject's past actions allows him or her to craft helpful suggestions that are more likely to succeed or, at least, less likely to be rejected outright at the risk of the hard-won rapport.

Giving advice should generally be held to a minimum and is best given when specifically asked for. It has many pitfalls in addition to those highlighted above; it can be experienced by a Subject as intrusive or bossy and can be seen as something to resist rather than consider. For Subjects with authority problems, it may well feel too controlling and prompt a resistance response. For younger, more passive or less resourceful Subjects or Subjects seemingly too tired or mired down in stalemate, to offer anything on their own, advice giving can be helpful and can unstick the negotiation process.

Resistance

It is usually a good idea to ask whether a Subject wants advice or not and abide by their response. Asking permission shows respect, an essential face-saving element of rapport and a key to enlisting a collaborative response. Where a Subject has said, "no," and their answer has been respected, they may feel free to accept advice anyway or later on – a perceived "trying to tell me what to do" is no longer a threat to their autonomy, and they can then agree to hear you out (the Negotiator). There are times and with certain Subjects that advice, as well as other interventions, is called for. Some expressions such as, "Help me. I don't know what to do. What can I do?" may be more about voicing frustration than a real plea to be told what to do. It is again appropriate to ask if they want advice. Whether they say, "yes" or "no," they may fear being "controlled," a common concern. Giving voice to their concerns can often soften or dissolve their resistances:

Negotiator: I know it feels like bossiness and no one likes to be bossed around, but it can't hurt to hear me out. Can it? You can still do whatever you want.
Subject: I hate to be bossed around. Don't push me. Go ahead. Say what you're gonna say, but don't expect me to do it just because you said so.

Resistance can be overcome by respecting a Subject's autonomy (in the end, the choice is theirs) and by exposing their fears about perceived threats to that autonomy (giving in is the same thing as caving in). Ultimately, a Negotiator may have to accept that the Subject will not allow him to actively guide the whole process. The Negotiator may be left to reinforce or challenge minimally. Doing so may or may not alter the course of the negotiations.

A judo technique (McKay, 1995) whereby the resistance is not pushed back but rather diverted or redirected (thrown over the hip) can be more effectual than "banging heads." In a similar vein, "calling process" (p. 164) is where the Negotiator turns the dialogue to what is going on rather than what is being contended, for example: "I feel like you are clamming up because you're angry at me for disagreeing with you." Or, "It wouldn't matter what I said now, you're just trying to prove something to me and it has nothing to do with what we were talking about." (For a fuller treatment of dealing with resistance, stalemates, and deadlock, see Chapters 2 and 5 and Slatkin, 2009.)

A Plan

The successful and desired outcome of the rational process of problem-solving – the generation of productive ideas, selection of one or more of them – makes up an action plan; putting into action, or implementing it, is the next step along the road to resolution.

SUMMARY

In this stage, ideas, options, other ways and means are explored with the Subject, the Negotiator acting to facilitate the process of problem-solving. Clearly, what the Subject has done so far has not worked, that is, gotten him what he says he wants. He has in all likelihood resorted to old, familiar, usual, and characteristic ways and means which may have once served him well or have never served him well. The Negotiator's goal is to keep the dialogue focused on finding collaborative solutions in the form of better coping skills, clearer thinking, better control over feelings, and sound actions; all of which culminate in an action plan.

Chapter 7

STAGE VI: DEVELOP AND IMPLEMENT AN ACTION PLAN

OBJECTIVE: "Develop and formulate an action plan" (Roberts & Otten, 2005).

A plan, in this context, has two elements, or is really composed of two plans: the first refers to the immediate plan to resolve the incident and lead the Subject and all concerned out safely. In developing a plan, the Negotiator and Subject have negotiated what to do, after the Subject has hinted at or shown a clear willingness to come out – the who, what, why, when, and where of it. It is all conditional at this point while the details are worked out – a subnegotiation in itself. Agreements about what the Subject will and won't do and, the converse, what the Negotiator (and authorities) will and won't do. Surrender details will be dictated by the SWAT commander. Some small matters concerning the surrender might be open to negotiation, such as, "I'll come out, but I can't put my hands behind my head because my elbow is sprained." The weapon is made secure by tossing it out first or by securing it by some verifiable means somewhere in the building. Where hostages are involved, their safe release is the first consideration; normally hostages are released first, either as a group or in ones or twos. As security is their primary responsibility, SWAT may take the lead and SWAT and HNT team commanders may negotiate with each other as the Subject and Negotiator negotiate in parallel.

Normally, released hostages are treated cautiously because their identities have not been established; hostage takers, and their confederates, may be hiding their identities and trying to sneak out by hiding amidst the hostages. For this reason, SWAT officers treat all exiting persons as unknowns. All are subjected to custody and search until their identity has been established. For this and other reasons, tactical considerations may take precedence at this point.

For the first element, the surrender plan – although it is generally recommended that the use of this term be avoided – the Negotiator must be more directive as he acts for the authorities responsible for custodial, safety, and security concerns. Much of it is more strictly a police procedural matter. Again, some minor changes may be tolerated. The strategy of the "illusion of control" is useful here. The second element or plan involves agreements made between the Subject and the Negotiator – the quasi-therapeutic – about what to do "after" (follow-through/follow-up). For example: talk to wife, go to the hospital, but not have to undergo ECT (shock treatment); enter a substance abuse treatment program; make restitution for property destroyed in the course of the siege; meet with probation officer and child welfare worker, etc. These constitute the conditional promises made by the Negotiator to the Subject over the course of the negotiations and that constitute a verbal contract for which the Negotiator is morally responsible. The Negotiator should never promise what cannot be delivered but is responsible for keeping the promises made wherever possible. The two elements or plans interact; a Subject must own the plan and begin to demonstrate his compliance or further negotiations become necessary. It is common for resistance or "buyer's remorse" to crop up during this the incident resolution phase. In some cases, negotiations must effectively be begun again.

The Negotiator's part in devising a plan consists of guiding and aiding the Subject, as necessary and appropriate, in coming up with a plan that all parties can agree to. In the end, the Subject must buy into the plan, even if somewhat reluctantly; the strongest buy-in is preferred. The Negotiator guides the Subject to draft a plan that takes into account realistic goals; stays within legal limits; includes a time frame; looks at possible and likely outcomes; considers and respects the rights of others affected by the plan. A plan that presupposes that an angry wife would be willing to forgive and forget without checking with her first is presumptuous and unlikely to succeed.

The plan may consist of each party's part, the Subject, the Negotiator, and the authorities. For example:

Subject: I'm coming out.

Negotiator: As soon as you are cuffed, I'll meet you with a pack of smokes.
SWAT Commander: If he throws the gun out the front door, we won't put him on the ground. Similarly, for the after-plan, the more personal and/or treatment follow through:
Subject: I'll go to AA meetings on the day I'm released from jail or the hospital.
Negotiator: I'll call ahead to let them know you'll be coming so that they can reserve a space for you.

The plan, in simple terms, consists of what we will do and what he will do. It is a plan that has been largely built by the Subject, with the collaboration and facilitation of the Negotiator, that is most likely to succeed. A plan that the Subject "owns" can be reinforced in a number of ways by the Negotiator:

1. Give explicit approval, e.g., "Good plan. You did good."
2. Have the Subject summarize and repeat the plan aloud (clarify any misstatements).
3. Remind Subject that the plan is a "contract" to be abided by and that everyone is counting on his or her agreed upon word to carry it out (tapping into a Subject's sense of honor and obligation).
4. Review Subject's analysis of "costs and benefits" of the plan to ensure that the Subject is grounded; and
5. Check out and test the Subject's resistances ("Are you 100% about the plan or do you still have some reservations?").

The plan remains to be Implemented – that is, carried out or translated into action – doing what was agreed to. In all cases where follow-up is attempted, it should be cleared and approved of by the command authority (in the Negotiator's chain of command); this is necessary to avoid the appearance of an improper or inappropriate relationship with the Subject. An improper or inappropriate relationship with a vulnerable Subject might consist of boundary-crossing or exploitive acts, to include: financial (transfer of funds, banking, investments), sexual, certain legal actions (hiring or paying for an attorney, seeking power of attorney), or undue influence in Subject's life decisions (wills, divorce). The above are improper because they violate the Subject's boundaries, exploit the Subject's present vulnerabilities, may harm their legal position, place the Negotiator in a dual role, i.e., police Negotiator and agent or representative of the Subject beyond the scope of the role of police authority. At the very least it gives the appearance of impropriety.

Should any of these follow-up acts have been committed to as a term of the Negotiations or as a simple act of kindness, permission requested and granted by the Subject must be witnessed and documented and have the approval of the Negotiator's superior officers. Such acts must be brief and simple and not go beyond the agreed to request, not involve illegal acts or impersonation (deception). Family or legal agents of the Subject, too, must be notified and any business beyond the circumscribed request turned over to them. The Negotiator should remove herself from the extended situation as soon as possible. Acts that may be appropriate might include transportation to a first AA meeting or to meet probation officer or direct to a college or career counselor, etc. The Negotiator should not allow any but an initial dependency to be part of the bargain. The Subject should be encouraged and reinforced for independent action; appropriate referrals to professional should be made for serious and/or continuing issues. Dependence should be discouraged past the initially agreed upon one, independence should be encouraged thereafter; any further dependency should be transferred to appropriate professionals.

Resistance was discussed previously. Here, too, it can assert itself as indecisiveness, delay, procrastination, passivity, and inaction. Common forms of resistance are seen at the juncture of talking about it to doing it. Again, resistance often leads to delay, last minute rebuke, misstep, or abandonment of the plan altogether. It can be due to: (1) distrust of authorities (paranoia); (2) insecurity or lack of belief in self (lack of self-confidence); (3) risk-averseness (ear of change, fear of failure); (4) ambivalence (not fully decided or convinced – of two minds); and (5) inertia (tendency to stay put). Even a good action plan that all have agreed to through tough negotiations may still have to be further negotiated or "litigated." And so, in the last minutes, when the resolution is at hand, any number of reasons why may be voiced or not. An opening strategy is to get the Subject to verbalize his "why" even if it is not the real reason – get it out so that it may be discussed; the Subject may not have a full awareness or understanding of his hesitation. It can usually be attributed to a feeling rather than a well-thought-out or rational revisit of the plan to which he, the Subject has already agreed. Active listening is again brought into play. Knowing the most common feelings that cause one to hesitate in the last moments, the Negotiator can quickly test out the most likely ones: anxiety, fear, ambivalence, uncertainty, insecurity, self-doubt, suspicion, loss of control, etc. The Negotiator might comment as follows:

Sample Dialog

- Is it that you are (afraid, nervous, uncertain, distrustful) about what is going to happen next?
- It's a big step. We all should pause a minute or two before we take the step.
- I explained everything that is going to happen. Do you want me to go over it again, one more time?
- Are you having trouble trusting – me or them?
- It's hard not to be of two minds about any big decision. It's perfectly normal.
- There's a time to think and a time to act.
- I know it's the right thing to do. In your heart of hearts you do, too.
- Is there anything I can say or do at this point to help you to do the right thing?
- You can do it.
- You are the only one holding yourself back. What are you feeling right now?

SUMMARY

A plan to resolve an incident might consist of two elements: (1) what, why, when, where, and how to exit the incident scene, release hostages, dispose of weapon, etc.; and (2) any post-resolution follow-up agreed to by the Subject, Negotiator, and authorities, e.g., bring my wife to the scene, get me a pack of cigarettes, meet me at the hospital and tell the doctor I won't allow shock treatment, etc.

A plan negotiated must then be implemented. Many times a Subject may hesitate at the last minute for any number of reasons, e.g., ambivalence, distrust, doubt, fear, anxiety. Active listening is once again employed to bring into awareness and out into the open where it may again be ventilated and processed.

Chapter 8

STAGE VII: FOLLOW-UP

OBJECTIVE: "Follow-up plan and agreement" (Roberts & Otten, 2005).

This stage is more relevant to critical incidents that do not involve criminal acts. Where a criminal act(s) has been committed by the Subject, custody and adjudication in the criminal justice system are the usual consequence; follow-up, as such, is provided through that system. For mentally ill or highly emotionally disturbed Subjects, once in custody, hospitalization on a 72-hour emergency hold or mental inquest warrant is consequential. Follow-up is largely in the hands of the custodial agency; however, some indirect follow-up with the cooperation and coordination of the agency may be allowed for. For example, a promised phone call to the parole officer to pass along certain information can be effected.

In incidents that have room for some discretion, a Negotiator and Subject may have agreed, as part of the plan to end the siege, to some negotiated preconditions – legitimate promises made that were instrumental in getting the agreement. Such agreements to follow-up must have been approved by commanders, by convention, and at the appropriate level, by the convening authorities. While the police may approach a prosecutor to apprise his office of mitigating matters concerning a particular Subject, as agreed to, the Negotiator cannot have promised to get the courts to undercharge anyone. Any follow-up undertaken must be transparent and witnessed, not only to reassure the Subject, during the tenuous time during negotiations, but to protect the Negotiator from the appearance of overreach and impropriety.

Follow-up on promises made in the course of negotiations can be seen as follow-through or follow-up. Follow-through pertains to promises made during negotiations that can reasonably be expected to be completed during the course of negotiations ("Send in a pack of smokes and I'll let the lady go." "Deal.") or immediately following the surrender, e.g., "I'll call your wife and let her know where to reach you. I'll tell the ER docs you can't tolerate Haldol." Follow-up, for our purposes, is used to describe the fulfillment of promises made that apply to deeds to occur less immediately after the incident is resolved and the Subject is restrained, e.g., "If it is OK with the docs, I'll look in on you next week. Historically, one rationale for following through or following up has been that the police may well encounter the same Subject again, down the road, in a similar situation. Credibility gained or lost here may color the Subject's receptiveness to future Negotiators, or to police in general, should negotiations or other police encounters occur in the future. Beyond the purely practical consideration above, promises made in good faith should be kept whenever and wherever possible. For this reason, promises should not be made lightly. Promises should be grounded and crafted to reflect limitations and likelihoods. Obvious exceptions to this duty are deliberate lies told strategically or tactically with the aim of resolution in the face of stalemate or deadlock, for example.

The limits to follow-up should be clear to the Negotiator (boundaries) and made clear to the Subject so as to avoid failed expectations ("I thought you and I were gonna be friends. You know, go bowling and stuff."). Perceived betrayal can be devastating to a Subject to whom a promise was made that he or she understood differently from what the Negotiator meant. Follow-up promises made should be:

- *conditional* (If it's OK with your doctor.)
- *delimited* (I can only promise one visit. That's all my bosses will allow.)
- *reasonable* (I'll bring you a couple of packs of smokes, but no more. OK?)
- *defined* (I'm glad we could work this out. You're OK, but that doesn't mean we can be friends. Ours is a professional relationship – friendly but not friends.)
- *legal* (HIPPA rules mean that your treating physician and all other hospital staff won't be able to talk to me about you and how you're getting along. Your lawyer may not want you to talk to me

at all or, at the very least, only if he is present. Appropriate follow-up might be limited to verbally transferring cogent information to hospital personnel, though another police authority, to a social worker.)

SUMMARY

Follow-up, an action usually more fitting for Subjects with crises related to other than criminal acts that are at their center. Its use has usually been associated with medical, psychiatric, and psychological referral and entree into treatment to ensure continuity of care. However, there is some discretionary room in any crisis negotiation to sort out terms of its resolution – or grand bargain. All parties may have to give something to get something, and follow-up/follow-through is the medium of exchange. Make sure he gets to where *asked* to go, e.g., AA; Gulf War vets group; and is compliant with the court-mandated, out-patient drug rehab program he is compelled to go to. Follow-up and follow-through may occur as soon as a Subject exits the incident scene (surrenders) or after the Subject is hospitalized or in detention. Because of jurisdictional rules, department SOP, it must be transparent, witnessed, appropriate, approved, reasonable, within bounds, and conditional ("if the hospital allows it"). Follow-up is not very common and may not be allowed for a Subject in custody facing serious felony charges. In any case, the Subject's attorney may prohibit it. Follow-up, where appropriate and within bounds, may be the fulfillment of agreements made between a Negotiator and a Subject to resolve a negotiated incident; such promises may have been instrumental in the resolution and the surrender contingent upon them.

Precontact: Negotiator prepares to engage subject.

Crisis team updates situation board.

Team intelligence officers contact agencies and persons related to subject and situation.

Ongoing negotiations: Primary negotiator engages subject as secondary negotiator coaches.

Jail special operations response team (SORT) goes tactical.

Postincident: First responder firefighters and EMS medics debrief.

Negotiations underway.

Domestic hostage situation: HNT officer debriefs released child hostage.

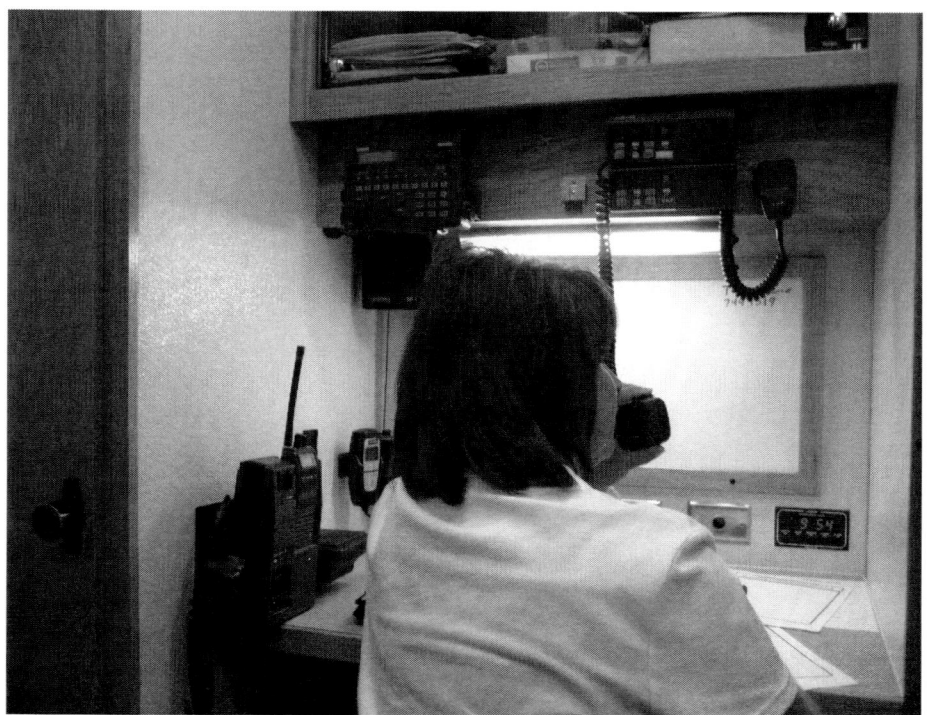
Crisis team's communications officer updates CNT and SWAT commanders.

HNT mobile negotiation operations center (NOC).

PART II

HOSTAGE, BARRICADE, AND SUICIDAL SUBJECT NEGOTIATIONS

INTRODUCTION

The following chapters examine some means of dealing with the specific crises of hostage taking, suicide intervention, and *barricaded* Subjects. Most of the means for managing kidnapping and institutional disorders also apply, although there are significant differences. You will note the essential similarities between the events and the Negotiator approaches as the specific situations share most of the same dynamics. Power and control are the watchwords and must be dealt with in these situations with these Subjects, in particular. Hostage takers, barricaded, and suicidal Subjects have externalized their inner conflicts and projected them onto the authorities: the situation they have created has placed them in direct conflict with the police or corrections officials.

Hostage takers, barricaded, and suicidal Subjects wrest with the authorities over what they, the Subjects, will or will not do; it is a struggle that, apart from their spoken plans or demands, is a complicated tangle or ego, feelings of powerlessness and inadequacy, hopelessness and helplessness, and misguided and misdirected frustration and anger over their dealings with the world. It is largely about who has the power and is in control. Power and control issues are present and to be expected; they constitute a major part of the negotiations and successful management of this dimension is the key to a successful resolution.

Here, hostage takers, barricaded, and suicidal Subjects are reframed to be viewed and treated as if they were crisis Subjects. In fact, I believe that they are, and that reframing them as such is not a big reach. As advanced elsewhere, these Subjects are twice in crisis: once, because of their choice to play out their personal drama in this way, and, again, because the situation they have put themselves in is indeed a crisis involving a police response, the only way out of being through negotiations.

Chapter 9

HOSTAGE SITUATIONS AS CRISIS NEGOTIATIONS

> If you talk to a man in a language he understands, that goes to his head. If you talk to him in his language, that goes to his heart.
>
> Nelson Mandela

For law enforcement authorities facing a hostage situation in which threats of violence and the risk of serious injury or death to innocents (hostages and bystanders), and public safety officers, there are few options: tactical assault, selective sniper fire, employment of chemical agents, and containment with negotiations. Hostage negotiations is the safest, most humane, and most efficacious remedy of all. Hostage Negotiators achieve successful outcomes in 95-plus percent of their efforts and without injury to any of the parties. Tactical assaults almost always led to injuries to one or more of the parties. Where once police officers, given to black and white world views and a drive for action and quick solutions over exploring feelings, most now support contain and negotiate.

The few principles of hostage negotiations remain sound and are enduring and universal. Among them: time is on our side; over time stress and emotionality decrease while fatigue and physiological discomfort increase; law enforcement's containment, superior force, and resources give them the tactical advantage that ensures them a "win"; an incident must be negotiable (the Subject must want to live).

The key to a successful resolution is the same for all critical incidents – "good" communication – from rapport building on through problem solving savvy and into "closing the deal (resolution)." The use of another person or persons held by the Subject against their will and under the threat of bodily harm (leverage) differentiates it from a suicide threat but not from kidnapping or, in the FBI's nosology (classification system), "nonhostage situation" where a person is on the scene at the center of the action but may not be against their will or the Subject does not attempt to leverage them with the authorities; their presence puts them at risk nonetheless and therefore they must be treated "as if" they were "hostages." An incident well known to most Negotiators entailed a Subject, who when confronted by police, put a gun to his head and said, "I've got a hostage" (meaning himself). In effect, this *barricaded* Subject had one indeed as he leveraged his own life, the authorities legally and morally obligated to try to save his life from himself (unless or until he were to point the gun at police or another person).

Some hold that an incident must "be negotiable" in order for law enforcement to negotiate (McMains & Mullins, 1996); that is:

1. *The Subject wants to live.* If a Subject wants to die or does not care if he dies, then the ultimate bargaining chip is held by the Subject. The authorities are legally, ethically, and morally bound to preserve life. To do so requires that both Negotiator and Subject are committed to the same end – preservation of the Subject's life where possible. If we care and he/she does not, there is no basis for negotiations. *Counter*: However, ambivalence is almost always present (although it may have been worked through and is no longer operative) and affirmation of life may be rekindled. Negotiations may begin here despite the Subject's protestations in hopes of changing a Subject's mind or winning a delay (see "Contract for Safety," Chapter 10).

2. *There exists a threat of force on the part of authorities.* The threat may be implicit or explicit; the mere presence of heavily armed and armored SWAT officers would seem a little bit of both, but a Negotiator may choose to state the threat directly with some Subjects, e.g., criminals, "It's deal with me or deal with them." "They won't come in as long as we are talking in good faith;"

3. *There must be demands.* A Subject's demands are the bargaining in a negotiation – "I want my cigarettes now!" They are the tangible basis for working out a deal – "You give me my cigarettes, I let the kid go." *Counter*: It is arguable whether a Negotiator should prompt a Subject for demands to make the negotiations "negotiable," e.g., "What's it going to take from me to get those folks out safely." Some Subjects may

be intellectually dull or did not anticipate this situation's development and are unprepared. Also, it is either implicit or explicit for a Subject to demand that the police go away, "that this whole thing just go away." It's a basis no matter how thin. These "demands" may suffice to negotiate in themselves or may give way to other stated demands;

4. *The Negotiator must be seen as someone who can hurt the Subject but is willing to help him or her.* After a name and organizational affiliation, the Negotiator's opening usually contains the words "here to help or how can I help." Again, the Negotiator may make explicit the threat of force behind him or her;

5. *There is sufficient time to negotiate.* Negotiation may be a lengthy process and should not be rushed. *Counter:* However, never say never. A Subject, mindful of deadlines, may react very pragmatically: "Cut the crap. What'll you give me for these people?" At the risk of trivializing life and death situations, negotiation can be like a dance – a slow dance or a fast dance;

6. *There exists a reliable channel of communication between Negotiator and Subject.* Negotiations can be conducted under the best or worst conditions. Frank Bolz (personal communication, 2005) spoke about talking to a Subject in a dark hallway through a cardboard megaphone. Also, see Slatkin (2007) for a discussion of a one-way conversation with an electronic hailer or bullhorn. Of course, a reliable and secure phone is the ideal (see below);

7. *Physical location and means of communication must be contained and secure.* The authorities have secured the incident site by means of an inner and outer perimeter – the Subject cannot simply slip out the back door and effect an escape. A dedicated phone line has been established by means of a throw phone or cell phone or, through the phone service provider, the Subject's phone has been rendered incapable of calling out or receiving calls from any phone but the Negotiator's; and,

8. *The Negotiator must be willing to accept that the hostage taker has much of the control over decision making.*

DEMANDS

A demand – absurd on the face of it – is that the police "just go away" as if police can simply walk away from a criminal act or situation where there exists danger to the public (including the Subject).

Their mandate under the law calls for their intervention. They cannot pass on it. Some other demands, while not absurd, are just as impossible or nonnegotiable; they include sending in weapons or ammunition, additional hostages or substituting one hostage for another (and in prison situations, escape, the release of prisoners, weapons, and drugs). Alcohol may be negotiable, under certain circumstances, though not normally.

Demands may be "expressive" or "instrumental" (Miron & Goldstein, 1979). Expressive demands are mostly about a Subject's need to have his grievances and concerns heard and may range from the rational ("I want the world to know about how X Company pollutes the oceans. I want to talk to a reporter for the Nightly News."), to the bizarre ("I want all women to shave their heads and for the hair to be offered to the gods for world peace."). It is about being heard, acknowledged, and ventilation of intense affect.

Instrumental demands are more concrete or physical, e.g., escape, money, a motorcycle, improved prison conditions. Demands may be made about the immediate situation, particularly comfort needs such as cigarettes, food, and heat. In domestic situations, child custody, visitation, and righting marital ills prevail. Other demands may be about larger concerns and a "freedom package" (McMains & Mullins). The freedom package includes escape, amending prison time, remedying prison conditions, etc. Terrorists or political crusaders might seek publicity for their cause. For the depressed or mentally ill, demands might be for suicide (to be left alone) or frankly bizarre and delusional ideas (reverse the Earth's rotation). In most situations, a variable mix of instrumental and expressive demands co-exist.

NEGOTIABLE VERSUS NONNEGOTIABLE DEMANDS

As a general rule, all demands (to include deadlines) are heard initially as *possible* – never say "No!" This gives the hostage taker a platform to make his case, no matter how impossible, and to be taken "seriously" – an essential ingredient of rapport; they are, however, subject to lowered expectations, endless delay, decay over time, and being "kicked upstairs" (not me but the Captain says we cannot), ignored or put off. Deadlines are generally ignored by pushing through them.

Generally, in handling demands, Negotiator's do not solicit or suggest demands, demean or dismiss them, or give into without getting something in exchange (make them work for it); deadlines, often a part of the demands, should be ignored by talking through them. Negotiation priorities are understandingly about sick and/or injured hostages and the medical needs of hostage takers as well. Having said this, suggesting innocuous "demands" to an inarticulate and expressive Subject might bring focus to a confused and disjointed Subject and event; offering "smokes" and asking for anything in return can build goodwill in a stubborn Subject; a blunt refusal to the demands of a criminally sophisticated Subject may speak to a Negotiator's credibility (a test?), "You know I can't send in guns. Let's talk about what we can do, not about what we can't." Response to a Subject's demands may have to be crafted or customized rather than made to fit the rules; however, some rules must be ironclad, i.e., no weapons.

Over the course of the negotiations, a Subject's demands and changes in his demands reveal much about the Subject himself and the progress of negotiations.

Negotiable demands might include comfort and sustenance, e.g., food, drink, heat, air conditioning, cigarettes, and media coverage. Nonnegotiable demands generally include weapons, drugs, escape, prisoner release, and exchange of prisoners. Transportation, money, and escape are more complex and negotiating for them might serve the interests of Negotiators in that they may be negotiated but never given (McMains & Mullins, 1996).

Negotiation Strategies, Stratagems, Tactics, and Techniques

Strategies, stratagems, tactics, and techniques are the negotiation team's and individual negotiators' operational plans, methods, and means (for a fuller treatment, see Slatkin, 2010).

Strategies

Negotiation strategies are overall or longer term plans or methods – a blueprint, road map or design – to achieve a goal(s). Foundation strategies in hostage negotiations are *contain, isolate, negotiate*. Negotiation goals are to engage the Subject, encourage emotional ventilation, and build rapport, move the Subject toward problem solving, a rational process that explores options, ways and means of resolving the incident peacefully, and, on to ending the incident by plan and resolution. Other negotiation strategies might include the following:

Buy time – Allows reality to settle in, physiological needs to increase, emotions to diminish, and intelligence to be collected; it occupies the Subject and may lessen the chance of violence. Where the incident scene, such as a residence, has amenities, e.g., food and water, toilets, air conditioning, physiological stressors are reduced or nullified.

Lower emotional state – With the passage of time, after an initial increase and expression of intense emotions (ventilation), the emotional state can diminish naturally. Meanwhile the Negotiator's actions: engage the Subject, build rapport; distract the Subject from demands, threats, and deadlines. Active listening that focuses on feelings is attentive, non-judgmental, respectful, and non-threatening;

Collect intelligence – Critical intelligence about the Subject and the situation can be gleaned from the dialog with the Subject while the negotiation team canvasses, follows up on leads, and runs record checks. Building plans and other similar data are collected;

Informants – Informants, e.g., relatives, coworkers, mental health professionals, etc., are potential sources of information and/or may be developed as third-party intermediaries (TPIs); they are identified and interviewed through the above intelligence collection process; information is collected, collated, corroborated, analyzed, and integrated with existing information to be turned into actionable intelligence.

Tactics

Tactics are the methods or plans – the means – chosen to achieve the shorter-term goals, in line with the strategies. Tactics might include:

Impoverish the environment – Telephones (cellphone interrupters), electricity, food, etc., may be withheld to increase the pressure on a Subject; care should be taken and thought given to decide that it is a desirable tactic for this Subject in this situation at this time; it may be used to further isolate the Subject or to demonstrate the power of the police authorities;

Nonthreatening/nonjudgmental approach – A patient Negotiator listens and responds in a nonthreatening and nonjudgmental manner; this allows the Subject to ventilate while feeling acknowledged and heard especially with Subjects making *expressive* demands (principal concerns are grievances without substantial demands). With criminal Subjects and others making *instrumental* demands (concrete or substantial) also will voice expressive demands (in fact most incidents involve Subjects making both in varying degrees). Criminal, and perhaps, inadequate Subjects, may call for a more directive approach though it, too, should be nonthreatening and nonjudgmental;

Reality check – Lowering expectations (the President cannot be made to come here on such short notice and $10 million dollars in $10 bills weighs 2,200 lbs.) is done to introduce a note of reality to the situation; the satisfaction of his needs, and in his best interests, is through negotiations with the Negotiator – the outcome depends upon him (the Subject) and the Negotiator; further, the Subject is told that the police will not go away or come in, although they can and may if need be; and

Use of Third-Party Intermediaries (TPI) – The use of TPIs is a deliberate choice of the Negotiation team. Obviously, they will not be employed simply because a Subject demands to speak to someone, e.g., spouse; the Subject's motives are unknown and may be part of, for example, a suicide ritual or other undesirable reason. Where the use of a TPI is deemed a desirable strategy, he or she should be prepared and rehearsed as to what to and what not to say. Recorded messages can be better controlled and can be redone or edited if need be. Care should be taken before allowing a TPI to enter the negotiation process even if only briefly and for a targeted purpose.

Stratagems

Stratagems in hostage negotiations are tricks (usually verbal in nature), contrivances, deceptions, or plans for outwitting a Subject to achieve a legitimate negotiation goal. An armed, barricaded Subject agreed to surrender conditionally, he refused to go to the hospital, insisting instead on going to an "institution." The Subject saw a distinction between the two where none existed ("distinction without a difference"). The negotiation team quickly responded by playing off the Subject's distinction by buying into it; their response was to say, "I don't know. We'll have to run it past the captain." After a brief delay the Negotiator reported that he was able to sell the captain on the idea and got him to agree. This stratagem gave the Subject the *illusion of control* by pretending that they, too, saw the nonexistent difference (in fact it was one and the same) and then by giving in to his final demand; making a big deal of trying to convince the brass to give into his inflated ego and mitigated any loss of face he might have felt by surrendering. Other stratagems might include the *Negotiator* looking for an opportunity early on to meet a Subject's demand and "gives in" by giving up something that he was willing to give up anyway (*Structuring a Success*). This sets the tone and the stage for the important negotiations to follow – it says, "it is to negotiate." It is also a show of "good faith" that can be traded on later.

Techniques

Techniques are ways of doing something using special knowledge or skills – a method, means, manner, form – the how. *Active listening*, a major technique, is the very basis of negotiations – it is what Negotiators do:

Active listening – Active listening that is nonthreatening/nonjudgmental and respectful builds rapport, trust and good faith for a Subject, one of whose concerns is being acknowledged and heard (his expressive needs); the rapport between Subject and Negotiator promotes the Negotiator's influence over the Subject and is his (the Negotiator's) technique for moving the Subject toward greater rationality and problem solving, and toward negotiating his instrumental concerns (concrete and substantial demands, e.g., a getaway car). Active listening is a technique made up of techniques; techniques can be subdivided into *listening, action,* and *sharing techniques* or *responses* (see Slatkin, 2010).

- *Listening responses* include clarification, paraphrase, reflection, summarization, and primary-level empathy. *Reflection,* for example, is a rephrasing of the <u>feeling</u> part of a Subject's statement aimed at encouraging more elaboration and ventilation; in contrast, paraphrase rephrases the <u>content</u> part of a Subject's statement when focusing on feelings is not desirable.
- *Action responses* include open-ended probe, closed probe, confrontation, interpretation, and information giving. *Confrontation*, for example, is employed by a Negotiator not to confront the Subject but rather contradictions in his statements or actions, "I'm confused. You say you value life, but you are endangering the lives of those people in there with you."
- *Sharing responses* include self-disclosure, immediacy, and reinforcement. *Self-disclosure,* for example, is where a Negotiator re-

veals some personal information about herself in order to join with a Subject and promote a more open exchange – it is one way of saying to a reluctant Subject, "It's okay to talk about feelings, and, for example, "I understand where you are coming from because I, too, went through a divorce."

Stockholm Syndrome

In August of 1973, two men held four hostages for 131 hours in the course of a failed bank robbery attempt. The four were humiliated, abused, and repeatedly threatened with death, yet they developed positive feelings for the hostage takers and negative feelings toward the police who were negotiating for their safety (and simultaneously engineering their escape).

The Stockholm syndrome is "An unconscious and paradoxical psychological phenomenon by which the hostages express or demonstrate positive feelings toward their captors and negative feelings toward the authorities (Slatkin, 1997)." It must be emphasized that this phenomenon is an *unconscious* one and not a manipulative means by which hostages play up to their captors in order to curry favor and try to insure their safety. The syndrome is believed to occur in three phases: (1) *hostages begin to have positive feelings toward the hostage takers;* (2) *hostages begin to develop negative feelings toward the hostage takers;* (3) *hostage takers begin to develop positive feelings toward the hostages.* The third phase is believed to be advantageous for the hostages as it decreases the likelihood that the captors will harm them.

Strentz (1979, 1980, 1982) proposed that there were five factors that promoted the development of the Stockholm phenomenon: time, isolation, positive contact, hostage taker reactions, and individualized reactions. In a study by Slatkin (1997), time, positive contact, and social interaction were tested and the data analyzed. The findings bore out the significance of time (duration of the incident) and social interaction (the opposite of isolation) but not positive contact. Significantly, the Stockholm syndrome developed in only 10–28 percent of the cases – not a very commonplace occurrence. Its importance had been widely exaggerated; however, its development should be encouraged and exploited wherever and whenever signs of it become apparent: e.g., hostages express positive feelings toward their captors and negative feelings toward the authorities, and Hostage takers voice concern for their captives.

The Process

Hostage negotiations is a process that progresses through three stages: (1) building rapport and the ventilation of strong affect, (2) problem-solving, and (3) resolution (i.e., surrender). It is a logical and linear progression, although it may occur in a seemingly mixed-up order that circles back on itself. For example, an established rapport may be damaged by some word or action and have to be repaired; it might occur at any point in the negotiations. Some negotiations open with, "I'm coming out." The three stages mimic those of a traditional psychological treatment (i.e., Beginning, Middle, and Terminal) and are parallel in process. Simply put, a connection is made (however tenuous), stories are told (emotion driven), tension is eased, and problem-solving begins – a deal is hammered out – a plan is made, and, finally, the plan that centers on ending the crisis – surrender plus safe release of hostages – is effected.

Power and Control

Hostage takers are engaged in a power struggle from the outset: they may refuse to negotiate; they may hang up the phone at any time during negotiations; they may change demands at will; they may up-the-ante by threatening to harm or by harming a hostage, etc. Confronting a hostage taker directly is not a fruitful tactic. It brings the power struggle into the open and heightens the Subject's resistance. Allowing the Subject some control (he already has some as noted above) and sidestepping direct contests is more fruitful. Active listening and good faith negotiations are less confrontational means.

SUMMARY

Hostage negotiations downplays the hostages' importance (a stratagem) and focuses on the hostage taker. Negotiators employ strategies (use of TPI), tactics, stratagems, and techniques as they engage the Subject in negotiations. The goal of negotiations is, of course, the safe resolution of the critical incident, safe for all parties. Negotiations can be viewed as a three-stage process: they proceed from the *initial phase* where contact is made, ventilation of strong affect occurs, and rapport is built; on to the *middle phase* where problem solving is at the center – the content is, in contrast to the preceding highly emotional phase, rational – ideas, options, choices, and plans are examined; and, finally, the *resolution (or surrender) phase* where plans to release hostages and surrender to the authorities are made and carried out. Negotiator responses to deadlines and demands, negotiable (food, cigarettes) and non-negotiable (guns), were addressed. Not all incidents are considered negotiable and some guidelines are discussed. The results of a research study on the Stockholm syndrome phenomenon were presented.

Chapter 10

SUICIDE AND ASSAULT: DANGER TO SELF OR OTHERS

He who has a why to live for can bear almost any how.

                        Thus Spake Zarathustra, Nietsche

Crisis Negotiators may encounter a suicidal person whose intent is obvious – a call goes out: "Jumper on the Second Street bridge" or a hostage or barricade situation in which the suicidal intention of the Subject is intimated or made explicit over the course of the negotiations: an oblique, or more subtle statement, such as "Not seeing my daughter is too much to bear" or, an overt, "I'm going to end it all" might be uttered. In the absence of verbalizations, a Subject's behavior, again, subtle intimations or clear actions may signal intent. Verbal statements or the intention behind such acts must be clarified as they may not, in fact, be suicidal statements. All suspicious behavior that suggests suicidality should be taken seriously; all such persons and behaviors are volatile – potentially explosive.

When a Negotiator clarifies or explores such statements or behaviors a dialogue is opened which can be both informative and therapeutic in that it allows for ventilation and intervention. Interventions may target the Subject's thinking, emotions, or behavior (Persons, 1989). An intervention in any one or two or all three of these spheres is likely to lead to a shift in the others. If a Subject's thinking is altered then his feelings and what he does subsequently are moved to be brought in line with the newer thoughts. For example, if a suicidal Subject who believes that he must kill himself, and his hostages, because he "dishonored his parents" by moving out of their home and taking an apartment with two college roommates, close to the school, can be shown (by reframing his thinking) that what he did is what young men (women) do to establish themselves as independent persons – a normal developmental task to be met and mastered by every young person as they move toward adulthood, greater responsibility, and the establishment of their own identity, prepare to launch a career, and eventually start a family of their own through interpersonal relations not under the close scrutiny of parents. A painful move, often, for parents and older adolescents, yet it is a commonplace, socially acceptable rite of passage in our culture. Such a new way of looking at himself and what he did should ease the guilt and cause him to reject the feeling that he is bad or wrong for what he has done and to feel more empathetically toward the innocent parties caught up in his personal melodrama. In turn, his behavior: the taking of hostages and preparation for suicide (stockpiling pills) becomes discordant – it no longer makes sense and no longer has to be. His life and the lives of the others no longer need to be sacrificed.

Where suicidal or homicidal intent is revealed or strong suspicions of such exist, the thrust of negotiations must shift – the focus, whatever it was on before, shifts to intervening to prevent loss of life. To intervene in a Subject's suicidal crisis by focusing on the thoughts, feelings, behaviors and, where possible, the underlying motivation or driver, the Negotiator has not abandoned the larger issues, i.e., safe release of hostage, but rather shifted to the core negotiation. Suicide crisis intervention is a meta-negotiation, a core negotiation. The larger hostage scenario, for example, is being addressed through the Subject's highly personal agenda, that is, the suicidal crisis is either driving the hostage scenario and is a "part" of it or it is a development of the frustrating and futile situation the Subject finds himself in. Either way, it is an important part of the larger situation and its amelioration will aid the resolution of the "whole."

The intervention begins with a lethality assessment – a prediction about the probability of the Subject's degree of dangerousness to herself or others. Only after such an assessment can the Negotiator know how to act next.

In assessing suicidality and homicidality (assaultiveness), the Negotiator should be respectful, direct, thoughtful, nonjudgmental, and, finally, empathic (empathetic). A Negotiator must listen fully before responding in ways aimed at heading off potentially dangerous behavior. While there are a number of demographic and statistical correlates (age, race, marital status), they are not immediately relevant in the suicide/assault assessment of a given individual. However, assessment information regarding a history of previous suicide attempts and gestures, violence or fighting as an adult, alcohol and/or drug abuse/addiction, careless or criminal weapons incidents, psychiatric disorder and inpatient or outpatient treatment, abuse and violence or suicide in the family, and poor impulse control. Immediate relevant concerns include recent losses and stressors, such as unemployment, marital separation, or divorce; loss of custody or access to children; serious medical disease or terminal illness; present psychosis, e.g., hallucinations and delusions; arrest for high-profile crime, sexual offenses, wide media coverage for a person with standing in their community; current alcohol/drug ingestion; depression with suicidal/homicidal ideation (ideas, thoughts, images, impulses); poor impulse control; and feelings of helplessness and hopelessness.

There is any number of reasons why a person considers suicide; some may be unknown to the Subject because he or she is subconsciously or unconsciously directed. Others are known and may be articulated by the Subject. Suicide is at its essence an attempt to deal with a problem. For the Subject, it is a solution to a problem; it seems to promise relief from suffering (a permanent solution to a temporary problem), control over an out-of-control feeling or situation, or revenge on others for real or perceived hurts. Depression is behind fully 75 percent of suicides. Again, because the psychodynamics of human suffering can operate overtly or covertly, the depression may not be known by either the Subject and/or family death investigators. The number is likely much higher than 75 percent, especially as there may be multiple determinants whereby depression is but one variable. Alcohol and drugs are associated with one-third of all suicides (Pope, 1985 cited in Persons).

In a self-harm or suicide assessment many questions may be asked, including follow-on questions to affirmative responses. Questions about a Subject's suicidal ideation, and mental state in that context should be posed directly and matter-of-factly without undue discomfort or hesitation (the Negotiator's discomfort, if present and detectable, can lead a Subject to withhold or deceive). Information from the overall "biopsychosocial" assessment is integrated into their risk quotient. Note: Subjects may be reluctant or may dissemble answers because of the fear of being pressured to give up the plan or the means or be hospitalized;

these fears should be confronted forthrightly: "In the end, the decision is yours, but, of course, I'm going to try to change your mind – you're not in a rational frame of mind and you should not be making such serious and irreversible decisions on your own – not now, anyway." The crux of this lethality assessment is: "Do you have (are you having) thoughts of death and suicide? Do you feel suicidal? Homicidal? Have you been, are you now, thinking of killing yourself or someone else? Have you been thinking of dying?"

Taken head-on, it seeks to determine whether or not the Subject is having suicidal (homicidal) thoughts – a logical and necessary place to start. Most importantly, it prompts a person to say so out loud, to hear himself say so and acknowledge it, and to confront the gravity of it – "an irreversible decision that will last for all eternity?" It is sometimes characterized as a "permanent solution to a temporary problem." A distinction can be made between active and passive thoughts about death: "I'm thinking about killing myself (active)" versus "I'd be better off dead (passive)." Active thoughts are believed to be more serious in that they may more likely lead to action.

Do you intend to act on those thoughts? A person may have suicidal/homicidal thoughts but be well-controlled and have no intention of acting upon them ("I feel like killing myself, but I am a faithful Catholic and could never do it"). You can and may have those thoughts because they seem to promise a way to ease or stop the pain you feel. Voicing such feelings can ease tension ("There. I said it!").The question then is: "Do you think you'll do it? I know you feel that way, but do you intend to do it?"

Do you have a plan? This question asks whether the Subject has given sufficient thought, coupled with his intent, enough to craft a plan. It attempts to ascertain if there is a plan and what it is; knowing the plan can help determine how far along the intent has progressed toward being enacted and whether it is realistic and feasible. More detailed plans are more serious. Has it been thought out or is it an impulsive utterance, "I'm gonna kill myself." Is it grandiose, fanciful, or plausible and within the immediate time frame.

You said you planned to take pills (for example). What kind? Do you have them with you? How many do you have? Given that you have a plan, do you have – the means – the gun or the pills on hand? This question goes to the accessibility of the means or instrumentality and the immediacy of a suicidal act. The answer, "I've got a pistol at my mother's house in California (3,000 miles away)" tells us that the means are not within reach and the act is not immediate. Knowing the plan and the means allows authorities to attempt to neutralize them.

Have you begun to carry out your plan? Preparatory behaviors such as stockpiling pills, drafting a note, saying good-byes, purchasing a weapon, etc., are steps in the direction of the act of suicide. It may even extend to parasuicidal behavior – hesitation cuts to the wrists, ingestion of a large but nonlethal dose of drugs, and ligature marks that indicate "toying" with suicide without full intention of dying.

What is keeping you from doing it? This question goes to assessing the Subject's remaining ego-strengths, counters (blocking beliefs), and social supports that are keeping his or her impulses in check – those parts of the self that are sustaining life in the struggle between "should I or shouldn't I?" Suicidal persons are always ambivalent (of two minds or mixed feelings) and can vacillate between acting or not acting on their feelings as an internal debate goes on. For some, a definite and conclusive decision is reached; for others, an impulsive act may win out; but for still others, they may be swayed in the direction of preserving their life.

Some Principles

- Among the principles, a past history of violence toward others (assaultiveness and homicidality) or the self (suicide or parasuicide) is the best predictor of future similar behavior; however, its success at predicting future is not very good. As it turns out, law enforcement officers, and other criminal justice and school personnel, are somewhat better at predicting violence than mental health professionals. Such behavior, as well as a family history of either, or both, remains a strong risk factor, however imperfect, and should be factored in any assessment.
- An overriding principle is simply a commitment to stop the suicide, preserve life first, wherever possible; however, in the end, a person is responsible for his or her own life which may defeat your commitment despite heroic efforts;
- All threats must be taken seriously. A Subject with many parasuicidal attempts may succeed by accident, misjudgment, or new determination to "do it for real";

- Doubt or ambivalence (of two minds) almost always is present and can be worked with;
- Empathy, and the rapport that it engenders, is at the center of a Negotiator's power to influence, though not control, a Subject's thoughts, feelings, or actions. Without it, the Negotiator is powerless;
- Ventilation of feelings and getting it out in the open in a frank way without fear of judgment is essential;
- Negotiators must be able to confront suicidal persons in a forthright manner, a quality bolstered by personal security and a healthy and good adjustment to life. They know that the Subject is at the center of the crisis and respect for his or her (the Subject's) values and beliefs, not those of the Negotiator, is paramount;
- In assessing a Subject's likelihood of acting out violently (predictive probability) toward another, and to what degree, a modified suicide assessment where "killing someone" is substituted for "killing yourself" is employed, e.g., "Have you had thoughts of hurting yourself?" becomes "Have you had thoughts of hurting someone else?" An affirmative response directs the Negotiator to try to identify that person as there are legal and moral requirements for reporting the information to police, the courts, i.e., mental inquest warrant, and the intended victim.

Intervention Strategies for Dealing with a Suicidal or Homicidal Person

In conjunction with the assessment, the Negotiator needs to begin to intervene where there is reason to believe that the Subject is dangerous to herself or others. It should be pointed out that a lethality assessment is in itself the first intervention a Negotiator may make; it gives the Negotiator an opportunity to demonstrate his/her empathy; it encourages the Subject to confront his thoughts and feelings openly; it is a reality check and an opening to feedback and challenge; it interrupts what may have been an oft-repeated internal dialog and plan; it is a rapport and trust-building exchange between Subject and Negotiator who can be seen as nonjudgmental, noncoercive; and, it is a vehicle for the Negotiator to move the Subject closer to rational thought.

Contracting for Safety

A Negotiator should attempt to "negotiate a contract" with a Subject with suicidal or homicidal ideas. The contract may be verbal or written, and witnessed where possible, as if it were a legally binding agreement. Of course, it's not, but by structuring the event as if it were, the Subject might be more likely to keep to the agreement – it taps into our cultural values about keeping one's word as a matter of honor. The contract seeks the Subject's agreement to not act out violently against himself or another for a given period of time in order or for something to take place, e.g., talk to priest or counselor, release from the hospital, etc. Negotiating for safety is a valuable tool in preserving life in that with the passage of time and/or the occurrence of events a Subject's desire for suicide or homicide might dissipate. Negotiating for safety is a meta-negotiation, that is, a negotiation within the larger negotiation for incident resolution; a successful negotiation augers well for other successful outcomes. Ask the Subject directly: "Are you willing to make a commitment to not kill yourself for at least _____ or until _____?"

No-suicide contracts may not work at all with organically impaired (brain damaged or developmentally disabled) or psychotic Subjects, especially those where auditory command hallucinations are present and are instructing the Subject to kill himself or others. These Subjects may lack the capacity to enter into and/or keep such an agreement. Similarly, a very impulsive Subject may not be able to stand by such a commitment.

Sample Queries

- Will you promise me not to kill yourself today while those people are in there?
- Will promise to not do anything to yourself until after you've seen the psych doctors?
- Promise me you'll wait till you get out of rehab? Talk to your sister? Priest? That guy you served in 'Nam with, he knows where you're coming from?

Interrupt the Plan by Removing the Means

Where a Subject has revealed the means by which she plans to affect her death, and has access to it, a strenuous effort to secure the means, e.g., gun, pills, must be made. To do so is to interrupt the serial drama that may insure their safety in the short term; too, it may relieve their anxiety in knowing that they cannot go ahead with the plan (it is an alliance with that ambivalent part of them that is not committed to acting on their impulse – their will to live). The means chosen are another indicator of the seriousness of the Subject's intent (more lethal).

Sample Queries

- Will you pass the gun out (pills, rope)? I'll keep it safe and you, too, along with it?
- Where is it? If it's not here can I have permission to have an officer get it from . . .?
- You said Tuesday is the planned day. The bosses are going to still have to put you in hospital or detention.

Encourage Ventilation Cautiously

Ventilation is a double-edged sword; it can release the emotional tension behind a Subject's violent thoughts or it can "liberate" them. A Negotiator must proceed carefully, gauging a Subject's limits (how much is too little, too much, just right?). Verbal techniques that slow down or speed up a Subject's verbal/emotional productions, e.g., open-ended questions tend to promote more verbal/emotional production, closed probes tend to slow down productivity; also, the Negotiator's own rate of speech can increase or decrease a Subject's (see Chapter 2).

A key component in suicidality and, probably homicidality, is the presence of *feelings of hopelessness and helplessness* – things won't change or get better and I can't do anything about it. Strategically, efforts can be made by the Negotiator to supplant hopelessness and helplessness with hopefulness and efficacy – you have reasons to live, things can change even if you have not yet found a way, you can fix some things (though not all) even if you have not yet found a way, you have done it before and, in any case, you can find the strength to go on nonetheless. Negotiators should guard against giving false hope and bromides (commonplace or tiresome "chestnuts"). Be especially careful of religious references unless you have determined a Subject's faith and belief system; it is likely that religious Subjects may have already tried to find answers in their creed and may resent your intrusion even if you are of the same faith. Ask permission and tread carefully. However, religion may be a fruitful avenue to follow. Check it out first to avoid rapport busting intrusiveness and offense.

Sample Queries

- Are there touchy things – you know – certain feelings or stuff I should probably tread carefully around?
- Religion can be touchy for some. Do you think of yourself as religious, a lot or a little? What does your religion say about suicide and afterlife? Would you be more comfortable talking to a clergy man (priest, minister, rabbi, imam) if I can arrange it?' I think you may already know what he would say.

Reality versus Fantasy

A strong dose of reality may be an effective technique with some Subjects, especially if they have made mention of hating the sight of blood or other expression of disgust. Describing the image of brains splattered on the walls and furniture from a head shot, for example, is graphic and likely not what the Subject had pictured nor wants to contemplate.

The Subject may not realize the pain and suffering will be great for those left behind (survivors) and that his or her suicide increases the likelihood that their children too may choose suicide. Too, suicide is a "permanent solution to a temporary problem"; while a cliché, by now it advances the idea that depression and other causes of suicidal thinking can change, as can she (the Subject). Problems are part of real life not the fantasy world of television (reality versus fantasy). Such interventions can move a Subject from fantasy and feelings to reality and rational-problem solving thought.

Sample Queries

- Have you ever seen what police officers and EMTs come upon after a suicide – the splattered brain and guts on the floors and wall – what of those left to clean it up and try to live there after it? The guilt, the pain?
- Your thinking is not clear right now, you're feeling what you're feeling intensely, but we all have problems and problems can be solved and we can get past them. Yes, there will be consequences for today but they, too, can be dealt with.

- I know people who have found ways out of and gotten through seriously bad times, against great odds. Do you know or know of people who have overcome great odds to win out in the end?
- What would a win look like for you today?

Explore Alternatives

People in distress may say that they have tried "everything," but, of course, they have not. By exploring what the Subject has done (and has not), the Negotiator may highlight new ideas; by so doing, the Negotiator communicates that there is still hope, that a solution (help) may be found. Again, it promotes rational thinking and gives pause to impulsive action.

A principal opening strategy in helping Subjects to seek alternatives is to suggest, to a suicidal Subject, that he/she may have missed some; it is a challenge to the absurdity that "everything" could have been tried; commonly, people do the same thing over and over again. "What have you tried? Did it help?" Knowing what was tried and what succeeded or failed helps the Negotiator to know what *not* to suggest as it would likely be brushed off with "I tried that and it didn't work worth a damn."

Sample Queries

- What would you think of . . . ?"
- What have you seen work for someone else – a friend, a friend's friend, a TV or movie character?
- What if you looked again at ideas that didn't work or might have worked with a little tweaking?
- From what I've learned about it so far I think that a fruitful approach would be. . . .
- You have great _____ skills. Surely you could use them to come up with and pull off a winning way, don't you think?

An Instrumental Negotiator

As stated above, in a number of contexts, a number of times, the Negotiator who relates to the Subject in a caring, attentive, respectful, genuine, active listening mode, flexible, and open manner can come to be trusted and liked. Being trusted and liked gives the Negotiator the power of influence. We cannot control another person, but we can influence him or her and what he or she does if we have established a good rapport. Subjects do not negotiate seriously with someone they neither like, trust, nor have taken sufficient measure of (tested?).

Plumb Meaning and Purpose

Existential philosophers and psychologists deal with issues around mans' existence or being. Viktor Frankl, a psychoanalyst (Frankl, 1984), evinces that meaning and purpose are central to our existence – we need to have meaning in our lives to face life's trials. His own experiences of horrendous abuse and privation, his ultimate survival in Nazi concentration camps is a testament to his core teachings that having a purpose, a reason to live can give you the will to live in the most trying circumstances. He held that we all need meaning and purpose in our lives to face the inevitability of death and, that that meaning and purpose is specific to the person himself.

A Negotiator who can help a suicidal Subject to find some measure of meaning and purpose, or merely spark his or her curiosity about what might be meaningful in his or her life as he or she contemplates ending it in the moment, can promote a dialogue by which he or she (the Subject) can reexamine his or her thinking in this new context. Meaning and purpose need not be grand, as in World Peace, but more likely a more personal one: redemption, making amends, meeting responsibilities, etc. That is not to say that it might not be a larger purpose, e.g., a volunteer post in an urban literacy program. The key to this approach is to tap into a Subject's need to do something, be something, that is valued and that gives him a reason to live and overcome that part of him/herself that wants to give up and in to despair and death.

Sample Queries

- Were there things in your life that you always wanted to do but somehow never did?
- Did you ever read about or hear about someone who did or was doing something that struck you like "wow"?
- When you were a kid, did you have dreams about your future – what you wished or hoped or prayed for?

- Have you ever met anybody whose life you envied, that you wished you had?

Such questions and self-disclosures about your own yearnings and struggles through life and what meanings and purposes helped you through your despairing thoughts and times can shift the dialogue to a life review or inventory whereby accomplishments, failures, and hopes are sorted out and new meanings, new resolve can emerge.

It is advisable to know about a Subject's religious beliefs (ask) before offering a religious solution, e.g., trust in God or prayer. For the irreligious, such advice can destroy the rapport. For the religious, trust and prayer may have long been tried and given up on, or that their beliefs may not conform to the Negotiator's understandings.

Reasons to Live and Die

Like man's search for meaning, we all have things in our lives that are important to us – interests, values, responsibilities, loyalties, creed (beliefs–religious or secular). Tapping into a Subject's world returns them to the rational realm and opens up an avenue for life-affirming dialogue. They are put in touch with past hopes and future wants and needs. Free will, in this case, means we can choose to live or die – the ultimate choice. Having a reason to die may be more in the foreground in the moment for the suicide-threatener; after all he or she has been focused on his or her suicidal ideas to the exclusion of reasons to live. Challenge a Subject to cite a reason to live for each reason to die – like an internal debate "devil's advocate." Most reasons to die (not all) are the products of thoughts and feelings that derive from a depressive outlook.

Sample Queries

- They say you don't really **value** something if you don't proclaim it and live it. What do you value, what have you done about it? What could you still do?
- You told me your reason(s) for wanting to die; can you tell me your reason to live? Can't think of one. Think of one that used to work for you. What do you imagine other people say their reasons are? Does any of that fit for you a little?
- What's really important to you? Does what you are thinking of doing square with it?

Inculcating Hope

With suicidal intent, depression along with feelings of hopelessness and helplessness are its roots. Hopelessness can be countered in a number of ways. Easley proffers *Five Metaphors of Hope* (David Easley, MD, personal communication on 12/10/2012):

Hope is like:

- *A Bridge over troubled waters* – my time with you and care for you during this crisis is a like a bridge over troubled waters – to help keep you from drowning until you can get over and past this difficult time. I am strong. You may lean on me for now until you are able to stand securely on your own;
- *A light at the end of the tunnel* – I want you to see that there is always "light at the end of the tunnel" – there is a risk that it might be less than you would hope for or that it would truly be more – life is full of risks. In either case, once in the light, you may see things differently – more hopefully;
- *A Harbor* – I will harbor you during this stormy time and keep you safe until you are feeling more secure and are better able to care for yourself;
- *Counting backward* – I want you to understand that there is an end to this hopelessness and despair – in a sense you have glimpsed it by knowing the end;

It is:

- *My intention to wait with you* – it is my intention to wait it out with you – you won't be alone through this.

The cliché "hope springs eternal" can be useful if it is associated with a challenge such as: "What have you done to try to change things?" By going beyond what has been tried, a Subject's certainty that nothing can or will change can be challenged. He (the Subject) had not thought of "that" and cannot be sure that "it" would not work.

Reigniting Self-Reliance and Self-Efficacy

Exploring with a Subject his or her past successes, can help him or her to recall a time when he or she overcame difficulties through discipline, persistence, intelligence, etc., despite his or her feelings of despair and helplessness. Pride in success and renewed self-esteem can be recalled with the recall of the events of the past and the difficulties overcome culminating in a successful conclusion – how and when it happened and how they felt when it did. Realistic encouragement and reinforcement can energize a Subject in the moment to try it again with renewed energy and a positive perspective. Similarly, depending upon the Subject's age, maturity, and interests, a recall of fantasy events (movies, comics, graphic novels, literature, vicarious adventures of others) can be employed: "Did you see that Batman movie where he . . .?" Exploring a Subject's strengths can be used to prompt him or her to find a way to transfer (apply) his or her strengths from a past situation or application to his or her current dilemma.

By reinforcing a Subject's strengths, the Negotiator communicates his or her belief in the Subject's ability to find the strength from within to solve his or her dilemma – having made a mess of things he or she can right it. The Negotiator's realistic expression of confidence in the Subject can fuel his or her (the Subject's) self-confidence, self-reliance, and adequacy temporarily. You are not helpless.

Sample Queries

- What kind of things were you good at as a kid or young man (woman)?
- Did you ever get a trophy for some sport?
- Were you in the military? Basic training/boot camp? Not everyone makes it through.
- Did you graduate from high school, or get a GED? Not everyone does?
- What are some of the highpoints in your life? What are you proud of?
- Have you ever had a situation that you thought you couldn't manage but you did, tough as it was? What was it?

Subjects who are suicidal (or homicidal) are so in the moment (even if it is a long moment). They are not suicidal every moment and with every fiber of their body. Even those who seem determined to kill themselves can be reasoned with or helped otherwise. Thus: a suicidal person has doubts, is hesitant or ambivalent to a greater or lesser degree, consciously or subconsciously, about suicide – there is a healthy part of him or her that wants to be able to live; a Negotiator must find a way to ally him/herself with that healthy part of the Subject's self. A

Subject may act on an impulse or decision long agonized over despite efforts to make such an alliance. Ultimately, that choice belongs to him or her. Nonetheless, Negotiators intervene to decrease that likelihood in the immediate situation.

Power and Control

A suicide threatener may be exercising his or her power and control over family, friends, spouses, or lovers. He or she may blame the other for his depressed and suicidal state in order to make them feel guilty and/or to squeeze a concession from them ("Don't leave me."). A manipulation. Struggling for power and control in that situation can translate into a similar one played out with the authorities – a Negotiator. Do not get caught up in their quest for power.

SUMMARY

Suicidal crises are volatile and may go either way. In the end, a Subject may kill herself despite the heroic efforts of the Negotiator. A Negotiator's ability to feel empathy, and demonstrate (communicate) it to the Subject is the single most element of suicide intervention.

A number of principles are edified: take threats seriously, stop the suicide, remove the means, interrupt the plan, encourage ventilation, be forthright, empathic, nonjudgmental, and respectful. Intervention strategies include contracting for safety, encouraging ventilation, use of self, counterpose reality and fantasy, explore alternatives, plumb the meaning and purpose of life for the Subject, explore reasons to live, and inculcate hope and feelings of greater adequacy. Central to intervention with a suicidal person remains the rapport between Negotiator and Subject – the quality of that relationship dictates the amount of influence a Negotiator has over a Subject.

Chapter 11

BARRICADED SUBJECT SITUATIONS

A Subject may barricade himself, usually at home, although it might also be at work or almost anyplace else when circumstances arise that prompt a Subject to choose to defy the police. He may wall off himself from consequences or capture. Most incidents seem to occur in the course of officers attempting to serve a criminal or civil warrant. Also, a criminal act interrupted by the police might prompt a Subject to try to flee apprehension; finding himself without an avenue of escape (or by plan) the Subject chooses to barricade himself in place in a room or building (industrial, commercial, or residential). In either case, the Subject seeks to resist police authority by pretending not to be there, refusing to respond or openly defying police authority or by demanding that the police just simply "go away and leave me alone." A mentally ill or developmentally disabled Subject may simply be overwhelmed and frightened by the events and seek refuge by hiding in plain sight.

In some barricade situations, the Subject may claim to have a weapon and threaten to use it (some leverage may be gained as police are careful and would rather err on the side of caution), or indeed, brandish one and fire at the police or bystanders.

An essential element of the barricaded Subject situation is the absence of hostages. The Subject lacks the leverage of using others to trade for satisfaction of his demands which, again usually consist of demanding to be left alone – one of the things that the police cannot do because of their legal mandate (the duty to protect). Ironically, some *barricaded* Subjects discover that even without hostages, they may leverage their position because the police have a duty to protect that includes them; threatening to kill themselves can be construed as a quasi-hostage situation, "If you don't do what I want then, I'll kill myself" (I am a hostage).

Many barricade situations, other than those of criminals trying to avoid apprehension, are driven by highly emotional states, particularly: fear, anxiety, anger/rage, depression, frustration, and defiance. They may be precipitated by an incident (domestic violence), a series or an agglomeration of like or disparate grievances, or a rash act (the straw that broke . . .).

Considerations

A barricade situation usually does not involve hostages (a non-hostage situation). The barricaded individual does not *need* anything from the police. In fact, his demands usually are simply for the police to go away. Further demands are of the expressive kinds, that is, "I have been wronged." "Nobody will listen to me." Their goal is to be acknowledged and to have their say – tell their story – consequently they may demand to speak to a corporate CEO, the media, the Governor; these demands (and goals) may not be substantive (concrete) and might even be unrealistic or bizarre, e.g., "I want the President of the United States to apologize to me personally." "I won't come out until barking dogs say what's on their minds." They are emotional – predominately driven by anger, frustration, fear, rage – and may be frankly paranoid. Rarely is there an escape demand as their goals lead them to seek redress of their grievances – they want to step up on their soapbox and have their say – they often do not consider their current acts as illegal and so, escaping custody is not even in their thoughts.

The focus then remains on their needs – the need to be heard fully and acknowledged without scorn (judgment and disapproval). Because the Subject's demands are expressive, the Negotiator must relinquish some control as he (the Negotiator) listens actively, allows the rapport to build and then exerts his influence toward rational thinking and problem solving, and resolution. As in any similar situation, the Negotiator's goals are preservation of life, apprehension, and recovery and protection of property; these goals are best attained through negotiation, principally by attending to those intense feelings and emotions that are driving the Subject and have precipitated the incident. Negotiation here means active listening, attending to feelings, which once ventilated, can give way to problem solving and, in time, resolution. Principal among the intense emotions associated with public acting out are:

1. *Fear* – Fear of consequences for acts or behaviors for which the Subject feels guilty, remorseful, or defiantly justified may drive this Subject. Fear of harm from police (immediate), or from victims and their relatives (later), or a vengeful God (in an afterlife), too, may enter his or her fear quotient; so too for irrational and/or bizarre fright (aliens?) – much harder to counter.

2. *Anxiety* – Anxiety underlies most self-defeating and self-destructive acts; it manifests itself as excessive/obsessive worry about past or future events; it clouds judgment, drives impulsiveness or, conversely, paralyzes the Subject into inaction.

3. *Anger/rage* – Anger may be in reactions to real or perceived ills or wrongs a Subject may feel; they may be relatively recent or long standing, mild or intense. Rage is an intense anger that may have grown explosive, having been suppressed and left to feed on itself over time before blasting open, suddenly and violently; rage may be directed at the self (self-hatred), other persons (spouses, employers), or institutions or corporate entities (banks, government, world order);

4. *Depression* – Extremes of low mood can lead to a Subject's feelings of hopelessness and helplessness, poor judgment, suicidal thoughts; barricading and publicly expressing their ills may be an act of desperation. At the opposite end of the depression spectrum is mania, characterized by boundless energy, unrealistic self-appraisal, grandiosity, poor judgment, and impulsiveness.

5. *Frustration* – Frustration is what a Subject may feel when obstacles or barriers block his chosen path, e.g., marital reunion. The Subject is at a loss for what to do next or instead, and may then show bad judgment, act precipitously, and believe that exploding – acting out his or her intense feelings is the only thing left for him to do.

6. *Other* – Mentally ill or developmentally disabled Subjects may be confused or under the sway of psychosis or be intellectually inadequate to cope otherwise. They may little understand their own actions and might be at a loss to explain them, much less explain what they hoped to accomplish by acting as they have. Alcohol or drugs may fuel a Subject's senseless acts, barricading being one such event.

Further Considerations

Construing the barricade situation *as if* it were a hostage situation is not so far-fetched. Hostage situation or barricade situation, the Negotiator focuses on the Subject – he is the key to the incident's resolution. That is not to say that in hostage situations our main concern is not the hostages, it is a traditional negotiation strategy whereby concern for the hostages is downplayed in order to deceive the Subject about their value and thereby diminish his perceived power. If their (the authorities') concern is so great, the Subject perceives his hand as even greater – they'll do anything to protect those people. We wish to demonstrate to the barricaded Subject that we are as concerned about his welfare *as if* he were a hostage – someone caught up in his (the Subject's) struggle. We attach to him the importance we deliberately withhold from hostages.

In complicated situations – a crisis whereby the Subject has boxed himself (or been boxed in) in a place he will not *and cannot leave* except by agreement with the authorities who through the deployment of forces have contained him within an inner and outer perimeter – the Subject has a dilemma with few choices. He or she must choose what to do. The divided self says, "If I do this, then . . . , but if I do that then. . . ." Costs and benefits of each option must be weighed, although the decision may not be an entirely rational one.

For the Negotiator, an alliance with that part of the Subject that represents the more rational or practical self, or the irrational and emotional self that chooses to avoid a tactical assault (for whatever reason) must be made. One negotiates to preserve safety and security by promoting a surrender that is in the best interests of all concerned as it is more likely to be controlled and orderly. By casting the Subject as a valued commodity, i.e., as if he were a hostage, the negotiation precedes as it would were there actual hostages.

Strategies and Tactics

The police profile may be high or low, a deliberate choice believed to be the most advantageous in a given situation; a high profile demonstrates the containment and willingness to "go tactical," while a low profile emphasizes the willingness to negotiate. A mixture of both may be the best approach. A Negotiator might say: "We are here to help you to safety, to protect you from your not so clear-thinking-self right now. Don't make a short-term decision now that will only make it worse later. But we won't go away until all is settled."

While the strategy and tactics for hostage and barricade situations are substantially alike (FBI/CNU), there are some differences. It is worth mentioning both in this context:

Buy time – Allows reality to settle in, physiological needs to increase, emotions to diminish, and intelligence to be collected; it occupies the Subject and may lessen the chance of violence;

Lower emotional state – With the passage of time, after an initial increase (ventilation), in emotions can diminish naturally while the Negotiator's actions, at the same time, distract and build rapport through nonjudgmental, attentive, respectful, and nonthreatening active listening;

Collect intelligence – Critical intelligence about the Subject and the situation can be gleaned from the dialog with the Subject while the negotiation team canvasses, follows up leads, and runs record checks;

Informants – Informants, e.g., relatives, coworkers, mental health professionals, etc., are potential sources of information and/or may be developed as third-party intermediaries (TPIs); they are identified and interviewed through the above intelligence collection process; information is collected, collated, corroborated, analyzed, and integrated with existing information to be turned into intelligence;

Impoverish the environment – Telephones (cellphone interrupters), electricity, food, etc., may be withheld to increase the pressure on a Subject; care should be taken and thought given to decide that it is a desirable tactic for this Subject in this situation at this time; it may be used to further isolate the Subject or to demonstrate the power of the police authorities;

Nonthreatening/nonjudgment approach – The prime principle of negotiation with Subjects who have barricaded themselves is to listen as they harangue their grievances and ventilate their intense emotions; a patient Negotiator listens and responds in a nonthreatening and nonjudgmental manner; this allows the Subject to ventilate while feeling acknowledged and heard – it is at the root of all Negotiator strategies and tactics;

Reality check – By lowering expectations (the President cannot be made to come here on such short notice) and a demonstrable but low-profile containment, the Subject is introduced to the reality of his situation; the satisfaction of his needs, and in his best interests, is through negotiations with the Negotiator – the outcome depends upon him (the Subject) and the Negotiator; further, the Subject is told that the police will not go away or come in, although they can and may if need be (best introduced in the most nonconfrontational and matter-of-factly manner);

Active listening – Active listening that is nonthreatening/nonjudgmental and respectful builds rapport, trust, and good faith for a Subject whose principal concern is being acknowledged and heard (his expressive needs); the rapport between Subject and Negotiator promotes the Negotiator's influence over the Subject and his (the Negotiator's) strategy of moving the Subject toward greater rationality and problem solving.

Again, even where a Subject claims to want to die there exists a divided self – ambivalence (mixed emotions). In this case, the Negotiator's goal strategy remains the same – to form an alliance with that part, however weak or slight, that wants to live. The Negotiator follows a strategy for suicide prevention/intervention (see preceding chapter); however, if the Subject has not made explicit threats or taken actions that clearly spell out suicide, it might be prudent, at least initially, not to speak of suicide, but rather to make references to resolving things and "coming out" and "getting on with it"; it may be more helpful. The Subject may not be fully aware that his actions may be covertly suicidal, that is, if he continues on the same trajectory, then his options will lessen and suicide or suicide by cop might become more of a risk – fatigue, sustained containment, a sense of despair, hopelessness, and helplessness may make for poor judgment and impulsive acts including violence.

As in hostage and suicide threats, it should be made clear that the police will not leave, but that they are there to find a solution that works for everyone. It may be left unspoken, or made explicit, that all solutions must end with the Subject surrendering to the authorities. The Subject is then told that the Negotiator is the one he must talk to to be heard – the only one. It may help to explain to the Subject, briefly and authoritatively, that the police have a legal and moral obligation to "protect and serve" and that that includes seeing things through to the end that best serves everyone, their safety and security.

Where suicide does not appear to be at issue, a strategy of ventilation (everyone has grievances), rapport-building, and increasing rationality leads to influence. A Negotiator's influence on the Subject to alter his or her present behavior and come out peacefully is the crux of negotiations between Negotiator and Subject.

Where the Subject is a criminal (has a lengthy or serious criminal history or the barricaded incident developed as the Subject was engaged in a criminal act), a pragmatic strategy is the best starting point; the most common demand is to not return to prison or to dictate the terms of his subsequent custody, such as, "I won't go back to _____!" Being kept safe from police abuse is a frequent demand, too. Pragmatic negotiation points might concern charges, probation, parole, prosecutorial and judicial attitudes toward cooperative Subjects, and intercession with corrections authorities, etc.

Sample Dialog

For All Subjects:

- Have you thought about what's best for you now and for after?
- What would your _____ say to do if _____ (she, he) were here?
- You know the right thing to do, the smart thing to do. Will you do it?
- You will have to come out sometime. Now is the/your best time to make a deal about how.
- What will you do after we settle things here today?
- I know you want more for your _____ (kids, mother).
- A lot of what you have said can be made better when you come out.
- Don't make this situation worse by dragging it out or making more bad choices.
- Who do you trust out there? What would they tell you to do?
- I will assure your safety. I'll be watching.
- Everyone here knows how you feel about _____. Now is a good time to come out.
- Come out and see what's done about your issues.
- You've had your say. Now what?

For the Criminal Subject, or Any Subject with a Weapon:

- I can't promise you anything but that I'll talk to the _____ (prosecutor, probation officer, etc.), tell him/her that you _____ . That weapon doesn't protect you; it only ups your charges and increases the risks that someone, you or an innocent someone, may

get hurt. I know you don't want that kind of trouble.
- If this is your way of bargaining for a better deal it stinks. There are better ways that don't include weapons, threats, and fighting the police.
- Take the weapon out of the mix. Make it safe. Toss it out. Please, don't risk the lives of anyone, especially your own. You've got things to do before you go.

Subject Strategy

The barricaded Subject, because he needs little or nothing from the police, presents significantly fewer opportunities for a *Negotiator* to "negotiate" and, consequently deflects the influence or control a Negotiator might accrue through the negotiation process; however, the establishment of a rapport and the unfolding of a negotiation paradigm often follows despite the difficulty in doing so (or minimal need to). That the Subject does not need the police is not completely true. The police perimeter cannot be crossed (in either direction) without the permission of the police who control ingress and egress; accession to police requirements is a necessary condition to do so (come out with your hands on your head).

As stated earlier, the *barricaded* Subject can be approached and joined *as if* he or she were a hostage taker. More importantly, he or she is a person in crisis – the personal crisis that precipitated the current situation and the crisis of a very public incident that necessitated police involvement – and are better (best) managed as "persons caught up in life's stresses" than as criminal perpetrators (a principal tenet of crisis negotiation).

Power and Control

A *barricaded* Subject is in a struggle with the police authorities – they want him to come out, he refuses to. The eventual outcome is predetermined – he will come out or the police will come in. In the interval between the first police contact and the conclusion of the incident, a *barricaded* Subject will be engaged by a Negotiator. The negotiations themselves may satisfy the Subject's need for some measure of face-saving control. If not, effective negotiations, particularly active listening, can resolve the power struggle – whether the Subject is *instrumental* or *expressive* in his or her demands will govern the particular strategy. For some Subjects, a more forceful and direct approach and the flaunting of a tactical presence may be called for.

SUMMARY

A *barricaded* Subject can be reframed, for negotiation purposes, *as if* he were a hostage as well as a hostage taker; it is a productive way of proceeding with crisis negotiations. He is in a crisis, albeit of his own making, but it is a crisis nonetheless. Casting him, the Subject, as a person in crisis is not a far reach. Treating him as a person in crisis allows the Negotiator to follow an effective crisis negotiation model – ventilation, rapport-building, and increasing rationality (problem solving) leads to increased Negotiator influence over the Subject. The police are obligated to preserve the life of a Subject, if at all possible; they will negotiate for a safe and secure resolution regardless – legally and morally they must. The Subject is both perpetrator and victim and the strategy may blend the two or shift between them as appropriate. A blend of tactical and negotiation techniques presents a balanced approach. Strategies and tactics are substantially the same as with hostage takers with some obvious differences.

The barricaded Subject, because he needs little or nothing from the police, presents significantly fewer opportunities for a *Negotiator* to "negotiate" and, consequently deflects the influence or control a Negotiator might accrue through the negotiation process; however, the establishment of a rapport and the unfolding of a negotiation paradigm often follows despite the difficulty in doing so (or minimal need to).

REFERENCES

Adler, R. B., Rosenfeld, L. B., & Proctor, III, R. F. (2004). *Interplay: The process of interpersonal communication* (9th ed.). New York: Oxford University Press.

American Psychiatric Association. (1994). *American psychiatric glossary* (7th ed.). Washington, DC: Author.

Bandler, R., & Grinder, J. (1979). *Frogs into princes: Neuro-linguistic programming.* Moab, UT: Real People Press.

Copage, E. (July 29, 2012). Vows: Emily Mitchell-Marell & Ben Umanoy. *The New York Times Sunday Styles.*

Dass-Brailsford, P. (2007). *A practical approach to trauma: Empowering interventions.* Thousand Oaks, CA: Sage (down Internet).

Ekman, P. (1985). *Telling lies: Clues to deceit in the marketplace, politics, and marriage.* New York: W. W. Norton.

Frankl, V. (1984). *Man's search for meaning* (rev.) Boston: Beacon Press.

Flannery, R. B., Jr., & Everly, G. S., Jr. (Spring, 2000). Crisis intervention: A review. *International Journal of Emergency Mental Health, 2,* 2. 119–126.

The Oxford essential dictionary of foreign terms in English (1999, American Edition). J. Speake (Ed.). New York: Oxford University Press.

Lankton, S. (1980). *Practical magic: A translation of basic neuro-linguistic programming into clinical psychotherapy.* Cupertino, CA: Meta.

McKay, M., Davis, M., & Fanning, P. (1995). *Messages: The communication skills book* (2nd ed.). Oakland, CA: New Harbinger.

McMains, M. J., & Mullins, W. C. (1996). *Crisis negotiations: Managing critical incidents and hostage situations in law enforcement and corrections.* Cincinnati, OH: Anderson.

Myer, R. A., Williams, R. C., Ottens, A. J., & Schmidt, A. E. (1992). *Triage Assessment Form: Crisis Intervention.* (Retrieved December 28, 2012 from www.wefixfamilies.com/4781 crisis/triage.PDF).

Patterson, C. H. (1985). *Therapist self-disclosure: The therapeutic relationship: Foundations for an eclectic psychotherapy.* Monterey, CA: Brooks/Cole.

Pazar, J. (N.D.). *Triage assessment: The triage assessment system.* Retrieved December 28, 2012 from http://www.uic.edu/orgs/convening/IE-27.htm.

Pennebaker, J. W. (2011). *The secret life of pronouns: What our words say about us.* New York: Bloomsbury Press.

Persons, J. B. (1989). Chapter Ten: Assessment and treatment of suicidality. In *Cognitive therapy in practice: A case formulation approach* (pp. 176–193). New York: W. W.

Norton.

Roberts, A. R., & Ottens, A. J. (2005). The seven-stage crisis intervention model. *Brief Treatment and Crisis Intervention, 5*:4.

Ruderman, W. (Oct. 5, 2012). The jumper squad. *The New York Times.* Retrieved December 28, 2012 http://WWW.NewYorkTimes.com.

Slatkin, A. (May, 1996). Enhancing negotiator training: Therapeutic communication. *FBI Law Enforcement Bulletin, 65,* (5), 1–6.

Slatkin, A. (1997). *The Stockholm syndrome and situational factors related to its development.* Unpublished doctoral dissertation, University of Louisville, Louisville, Kentucky.

Slatkin, A. (July, 2000). The role of the mental health consultant in hostage negotiations: The incident phase. *Police Chief,* 64–66.

Slatkin, A. (May-June 2007). Negotiations with bullhorns. *Tactical Response.*

Slatkin, A. (2010). *Communication in crisis and hostage negotiations: Practical communication techniques, stratagems, and strategies for law enforcement, corrections, and emergency service personnel in managing critical incidents* (2nd ed.). Springfield, IL: Charles C Thomas.

Slatkin, A. (2010). *Training strategies for crisis and hostage negotiations: Scenario writing and creative variations in role play.* Springfield, IL: Charles C Thomas.

Strentz, T. (1979). Law enforcement policy and the ego defenses of the hostage. *FBI Law Enforcement Bulletin, 48,*(4), 1–11.

Strentz, T. (1980). The Stockholm syndrome: Law enforcement policy and the ego defenses of the hostage. *Annals of the New York Academy of Sciences, 347,* 137–150.

Strentz, T. (1980). The Stockholm syndrome: Law enforcement policy and hostage behavior. In F. M. Ochberg & D. A. Soskis (Eds.), *Victims of terrorism* (pp. 149–163). Boulder, CO: Westview Press.

Young, M. A. (1993). Crisis intervention. *Victim assistance: Frontiers and fundamental.* National Organization for Victim Assistance. Retrieved from the internet, Nov. 30, 2012. www.thecounselingteam/interactive/articles/crisis Intervention techniques.pdf).

CHARLES C THOMAS • PUBLISHER, LTD.

LATINO POLICE OFFICERS IN THE UNITED STATES
By Martin Guevara Urbina
& Sofia Espinoza Alvarez
2015, 290 pp. (7 x 10), 4 il., 10 tables.
$43.95 (paper), $43.95 (ebook)

CRIMINAL JUSTICE HANDBOOK ON MASCULINITY, MALE AGGRESSION, AND SEXUALITY
By Carmen M. Cusack
2015, 272 pp. (7 x 10), 20 il.
$45.95 (paper), $45.95 (ebook)

SIGNIFICANT TACTICAL POLICE CASES
By Tomas C. Mijares & Ronald M. McCarthy
2015, 276 pp. (7 x 10), 21 il.
$24.95 (paper), $24.95 (ebook)

Jones' AFTER THE SMOKE CLEARS (2nd Ed.)
By Adam Pasciak
2015, 226 pp. (7 x 10), 21 il., 8 tables.
$33.95 (paper), $33.95 (ebook)

PUBLIC SAFETY SUICIDE
By Mary Van Haute & John M. Violanti
2015, 136 pp. (7 x 10)
$24.95 (paper), $24.95 (ebook)

DEALING WITH THE MENTALLY ILL PERSON ON THE STREET
By Daniel M. Rudofossi
2015, 252 pp. (7 x 10)
$51.95 (paper), $51.95 (ebook)

CONSTITUTIONAL LAW FOR CRIMINAL JUSTICE PROFESSIONALS AND STUDENTS
By Kenneth Bresler
2014, 520 pp. (7 x 10), 26 il.
$79.95 (hard), $79.95 (ebook)

SERIAL KILLERS
By William M. Harmening
2014, 280 pp. (7 x 10), 28 il.
$39.95 (paper), $39.95 (ebook)

INSTRUCTOR POWERPOINT SLIDES FOR O'HARA'S FUNDAMENTALS OF CRIMINAL INVESTIGATION (8th Ed.)
By DeVere D. Woods, Jr.
2014
$99.95 (cd-rom), $99.95 (direct download)

INTRODUCTION TO CRIMINAL JUSTICE RESEARCH METHODS (3rd Ed.)
By Gennaro F. Vito, Julie C. Kunselman & Richard Tewksbury
2014, 276 pp. (7 x 10), 12 il., 6 tables.
$44.95 (paper), $44.95 (ebook)

POLICE THEORY IN AMERICA
By Robert C. Wadman
2009, 198 pp. (7 x 10), 18 il.
$32.95 (paper), $32.95 (ebook)

A STUDY GUIDE FOR COMMON SENSE POLICE SUPERVISION (5th Ed.)
By Gerald W. Garner
2014, 122 pp. (7 x 10)
$26.95 (spiral)

CRISIS INTERVENTION IN CRIMINAL JUSTICE/SOCIAL SERVICE (5th Ed.)
By James E. Hendricks & Cindy S. Hendricks
2014, 472 pp. (7 x 10), 5 tables.
$59.95 (paper), $59.95 (ebook)

DYING FOR THE JOB
By John M. Violanti
2014, 212 pp. (7 x 10), 7 il., 3 tables.
$36.95 (paper), $36.95 (ebook)

A PREPARATION GUIDE FOR THE ASSESSMENT CENTER METHOD (2nd Ed.)
By Tina Lewis Rawe
2013, 330 pp. (7 x 10), 2 il.
$44.95 (spiral), $44.95 (ebook)

MANAGING THE INVESTIGATIVE UNIT (2nd Ed.)
By Daniel S. McDevitt
2012, 236 pp. (7 x 10), 2 tables.
$34.95 (paper), $34.95 (ebook)

Find us on Facebook
FACEBOOK.COM/CCTPUBLISHER

TO ORDER: 1-800-258-8980 • books@ccthomas.com • www.ccthomas.com